# Traffic Signs Manual

Department of Transport

Scottish Development Department

Welsh Office

London: HMSO

# Contents of Chapters 1–14

© Crown Copyright 1985
First published 1980
Second edition 1985
Applications for reproduction should be made to HMSO
Third impression 1993

ISBN  0  11  550708  6

# Foreword

1. In 1963 the Traffic Signs Committee under the Chairmanship of Sir Walter Worboys, presented its report to the Secretary of State for Scotland and the then Minister of Transport whose responsibilities on highway matters at that time covered Wales as well as England.

2. The report recommended the introduction of entirely new traffic signs on all-purpose roads and suggested the introduction of an illustrated manual to provide advice and guidance on their use.

3. The new signs were first prescribed in the Traffic Signs Regulations and General Directions 1964 which came into operation on 1 January 1965. The 1964 Regulations have since been revoked by the Traffic Signs Regulations and General Directions 1975 which have in turn been revoked by the Traffic Signs Regulations and General Directions 1981.

4. It was expected that the Traffc Signs Manual would take a long time to prepare and publish and therefore the green booklet "Informatory Signs for use on All-purpose Roads" was published in 1964 to encourage the early introduction of some of the new signs. In addition to dealing comprehensively with the subject of Informatory Signs, the booklet included the design rules for the new signs and gave guidance on such matters as their mounting and siting. Although much of the information given in "Informatory Signs for use on All-purpose Roads" is still relevant, readers should now read it in conjunction with the revised design rules and advice given in the joint Departmental Circular No:— Department of the Environment Circular Roads No: 7/75, Scottish Development Department Circular No: R332 and Welsh Office Circular No: 54/75.

5. The manual itself was originally planned and published in separate chapters as loose leaf publications, for insertion into the "Traffic Signs Manual" binder. It was thought that this form of publication would facilitate the revision of the manual as and when required. Amendments and revised texts could be introduced simply by an exchange of pages. Unfortunately the amendment system has been wholly frustrated by administrative and distributive difficulties and consequently it has been found necessary when revising chapters or bringing them up-to-date, to re-write each Chapter as a whole. In these circumstances and to meet the needs of individuals and individual organisations whose interests may be confined to a single chapter, it has been decided to abandon the loose leaf format and to publish all revised and hitherto unpublished chapters when required as individually bound publications.

6. The chapter contents of the complete Traffic Signs Manual are listed opposite. The chapters marked with an asterisk are currently available in the form of individually bound publications and future publications of chapters of the Traffic Signs Manual will be notified in official circulars issued either individually or jointly by the 3 Departments concerned.

7. Enquiries regarding the Traffic Signs Manual may be made through the appropriate Director (Transport) or direct to the Highways Computing, Signs and Lighting Division of the Department of Transport.

*Department of Transport*
*Scottish Development Department*
*Welsh Office*

CHAPTER 5
# Road Markings

CHAPTER 5

# Contents

# CONTENTS

NOTES:

   1. The Traffic Signs Manual is equally applicable in England, Scotland and Wales and references to the "Secretary of State" should be interpreted as referring to—either the Secretary of State for Transport in England, the Secretary of State for Scotland or the Secretary of State for Wales as appropriate.

   2. References to the Director (Transport) should be interpreted in London, Scotland and Wales as referring to:— The Assistant Chief Engineer, The Greater London Roads and Traffic Division, the Chief Road Engineer, Scottish Development Department and the Director of Engineering of the Transport and Highways Group respectively.

   3. All sign diagram numbers quoted relate to the Traffic Signs and General Directions 1981, as amended.

   4. Dimensions shown in respect of any signs or illustrations in this chapter are expressed in millimetres unless otherwise specified.

   5. Whilst the Traffic Signs Manual gives general guidance on the implementation of the Traffic Signs Regulations and General Directions 1981 as amended, specific mention of the authorisation requirements for certain prescribed signs has been deliberately omitted from this chapter in anticipation of possible revisions to those requirements. Readers are however reminded of the need to abide by the Regulation requirements currently in force.

# 1.  Introductory

5.1 Road markings may be defined as markings on the surface of the road for the control, warning, guidance or information of road users. They may be used to supplement kerbside or overhead signs, or they may be used alone.

5.2 The markings have the limitation that they may be obliterated by snow, their conspicuity is impaired when wet or dirty and their durability depends largely on their exposure to traffic wear. Nevertheless, they serve a very important function in conveying to drivers information and requirements which might not otherwise be possible by upright signs. They have the advantage that they can often be seen when an erected sign is obscured, and, unlike such signs, they can provide a continuing message to the moving driver.

5.3 The continued increase in the volume of traffic using the roads makes an extensive use of road markings essential to ensure that full use is made of the available road space. In particular widespread use of lane markings is desirable; by enhancing lane discipline they add materially to the safety of traffic, besides improving traffic flows. In urban areas considerable advantages accrue from road markings at junctions.

5.4 It is strongly recommended that road markings be considered in detail at the design stage of new or improved junctions. The markings for existing junctions are often best considered on plan before the work is undertaken.

**Classes of Marking**

5.5 Road markings may be classified as follows: —
   (a) Transverse markings, which are at right-angles (or thereabouts) to the centre line of the carriageway.
   (b) Longitudinal markings.
      (i)   Double lines
      (ii)  Warning lines
      (iii) Lane lines
      (iv)  Edge lines.
   (c) Markings at level crossings.
   (d) Markings at roundabouts.
   (e) Yellow markings for waiting and loading restrictions.
   (f) Worded markings, parking bays, box markings and bus and cycle lanes.
   (g) Junction markings.
   (h) Markings at pedestrian crossings.
   (i) Hatched markings.

5.6 Each class is considered separately in later sections.

# 2.  Legal

5.7 All road markings need to be either prescribed by regulation or specially authorised by the Secretary of State. They may be laid only by or on behalf of the highway authority. It should be noted that "NO PARKING" and "SCHOOL" are not prescribed markings and must not be used.

# 3. Colour

5.8 The European Agreement supplementing the Convention on Road Signs and Signals and the Protocol on Road Markings, additional to that Agreement, (opened for signature at Geneva on the 1 March 1973) to which the United Kingdom is a signatory made provision as follows:—

"The road markings shall be white. The term 'white' includes shades of silver or light grey. However:
- markings showing places where parking is permitted or restricted may be blue;
- zig-zag lines showing places where parking is prohibited shall be yellow;
- the continuous or broken line on the kerb or on the edge of the carriageway to show that standing or parking is prohibited or restricted shall be yellow."

5.9 The United Kingdom has chosen white for markings intended for moving traffic, including borderlines, and yellow for waiting restrictions.

There are some exceptions to this general rule, notably, YELLOW BOX MARKINGS, SCHOOL KEEP CLEAR AND BUS AND TAXI markings in some cases. Blue carriageway markings are not used in the United Kingdom.

5.10 The standard colour for yellow markings is BS381C No 355 (lemon). In environmentally sensistive areas yellow markings to No 310 (primrose) or No 353 (deep cream) may be used.

5.11 Reflecting Road studs. Four colours of reflecting road studs are prescribed for use in the United Kingdom. These are:—
(i) White (or clear)
(ii) Red
(iii) Green
(iv) Amber

5.12 Details as to where the various colours may be used are given in Section 18 of this Chapter.

5.13 not allocated.

# 4. Transverse Markings

5.14 The prescribed transverse markings, comprise:—
(i) STOP LINES and
(ii) GIVE WAY LINES.

**(i) STOP LINES**

5.15 Two sizes are prescribed:—
(a) A 200mm (300mm) wide line (Diag. 1001) indicates the position beyond which a driver should not proceed when required to stop by the Police or by traffic signals, including signals at level crossings (see Section 9), swing bridges, or signals on roads adjacent to airfields.
(b) A 400mm wide line (Diag. 1002.1) is used exclusively at junctions controlled by STOP signs and should in no circumstances be used merely to give warning of the approach to a major road, for which the GIVE WAY marking is appropriate.

5.16 The significance of the STOP sign supplemented by the STOP line in Regulation 11 (1) (b) of the Traffic Signs Regulations and General Directions 1981 is as follows:—

(i) "every vehicle shall, before entering the major road, stop at the transverse lines shown in Diag. 1002.1) or, if they are not for the time being visible, at the major road, and

(ii) no vehicle shall proceed past such one of the said transverse lines as is nearest to the major road into that road, or, if those lines are not for the time being visible, shall enter into the major road, in such a manner or at such a time as is likely to cause danger to the driver of any other vehicle on the major road or as to necessitate the driver of any such other vehicle to change its speed or course in order to avoid an accident with the first-mentioned vehicle."

NOTE: See Chapter 3 for the significance of the STOP sign.

5.17 Both patterns of line should be accompanied by longitudinal warning lines extending from the junction in accordance with standards recommended in Section 6 for approach warning lines.

## Traffic Signal STOP Line (Diag. 1001) Figs 5:35 and 5:36

5.18 The marking consists of a single continuous line 200mm or 300mm in width. The 200mm width is generally for use in urban areas and the 300mm width in rural areas. The greater width may also be used in urban areas at difficult junctions.

5.19 At traffic signals the line is normally located 1m before the near-side primary signal, but site conditions may necessitate adjustment in this distance. Details of this marking are shown in Figs 5:35 and 5:36. At Police control points the line should be provided where the control operates for not less than 20 hours per week. It should be located in consultation with the Police.

## Junction STOP Line (Diag. 1002.1) Fig 5:1.

5.20 The marking consists of a single continuous line 400mm in width, and supplements the STOP sign.

The edge of the STOP line nearest to the major road should normally continue the line of the edge of the major road carriageway. Only very rarely should it be elsewhere and then it must be sited so as to halt a driver where his visibility is best. It should not be closer than 600mm to the path normally followed by the nearest side of the major road vehicles.

This STOP line must always be accompanied by the worded STOP marking on the carriageway. See para 5.131 for details of this marking and its siting.

Where advance warning of the STOP sign is required, this is provided by the advance sign (Diag. 501) and distance plate, (Diag. 502) in association with SLOW on the carriageway. Table B in Chapter 3 shows the circumstances where this is justified.

### (ii) GIVE WAY Lines

5.21 Four patterns are prescribed. They are used at:
- (i) major/minor road junctions Fig.5:2
- (ii) *conventional and small roundabouts
- (iii) *mini roundabouts
- (iv) level crossings (for pedestrians)

*As defined in para 5.112

Only pattern (i) is dealt with in this section. Patterns (ii) and (iii) are dealt with in Section 10 and pattern (iv) in Section 9.

5.22 The prescribed marking (pattern (i)) consists of 2 broken lines laid side by side, each comprising 600mm marks and 300mm gaps. The lines are 200mm wide and are spaced 300mm apart. Subject to what follows the marking is laid across the mouths of minor roads at junctions.

5.23 The significance of the marking as prescribed in Regulation 22 (2) and (3) of the Traffic Signs Regulations and General Directions 1975 is as follows:

"the requirement conveyed by the said transverse lines, whether or not they are used in conjunction with the sign shown in diagram 602, shall be that no vehicle shall proceed past such one of those lines as is nearest to the major road on to that road in such a manner or at such a time as is likely to cause danger to the driver of any other vehicle on the major road or as to necessitate the driver of any such other vehicle to change its speed or course in order to avoid an accident with the first-mentioned vehicle."

NOTE: See Chapter 3 for the significance of the GIVE WAY sign.

5.24 With the exceptions mentioned in para 5.29, the GIVE WAY marking is intended for use at all junctions other than those which are controlled by STOP signs, traffic signals or the police.

5.25 In view of the large number of junctions involved, it is suggested that they be marked in the following order of priority:
- (i) All junctions with primary routes.
- (ii) Other junctions where there are special difficulties which could give rise to accidents.
- (iii) Junctions with classified roads.
- (iv) Any other junctions.

5.26 On two-way minor roads, the marking normally extends to the centre of the carriageway of the

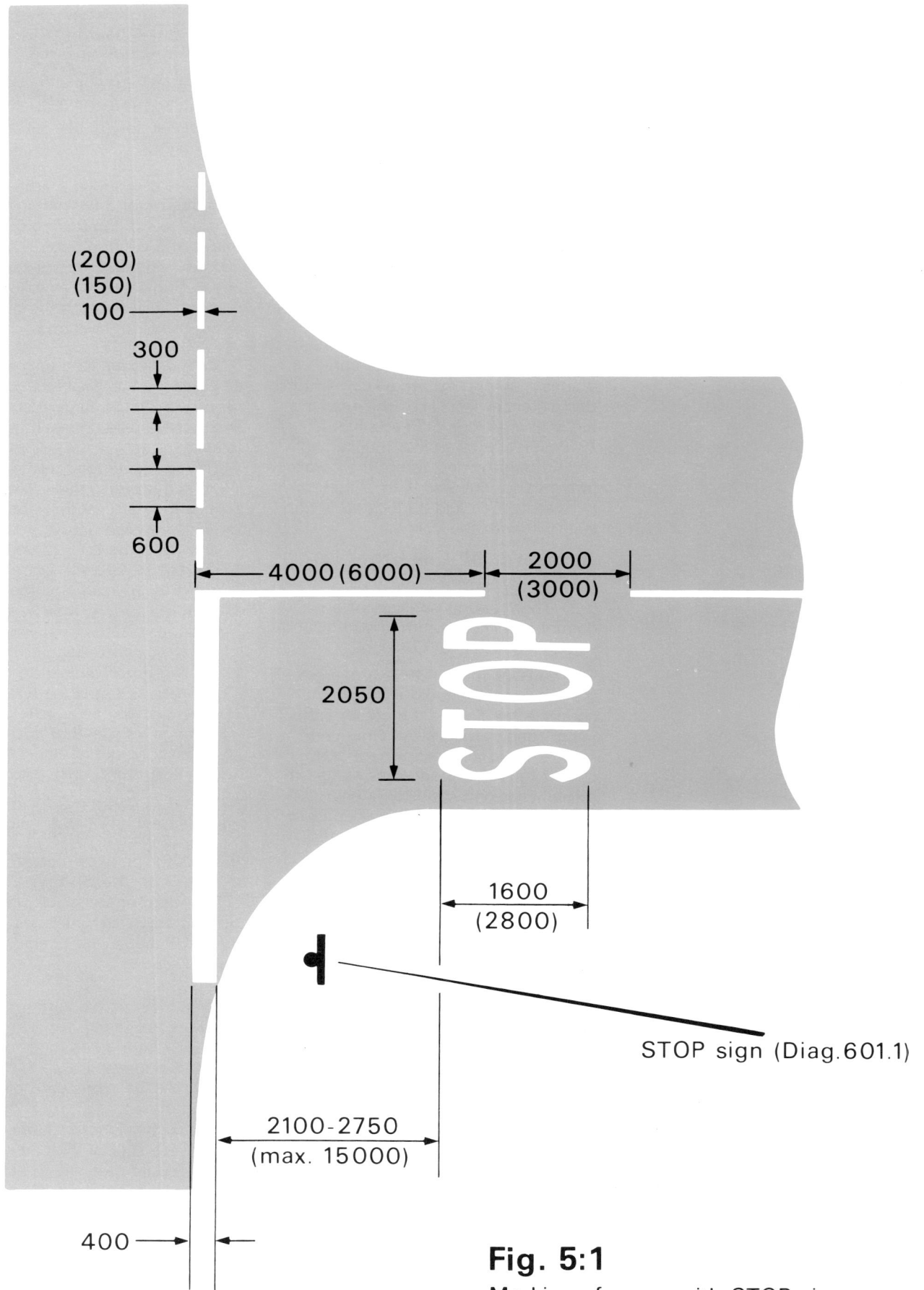

(200)
(150)
100

300

600

4000 (6000)

2000
(3000)

2050

1600
(2800)

STOP sign (Diag. 601.1)

2100-2750
(max. 15000)

400

## Fig. 5:1

Markings for use with STOP sign

minor road; on a one-way road it is carried across the whole width of the minor road. The precise location of the marking nearest to the major road in relation to the edge of the major road is governed by the same considerations as the STOP line supplementing the STOP sign (see para 5.20). On roads where a 1 metre, strip is provided, again the transverse GIVE WAY marking should be positioned to continue the edge of the major road carriageway and not in line with the edge of carriageway marking. (see Fig 5:3a).

5.27 Where the application of the above rules would result in a line less than 2.75m long, the marking should be carried right across the road.

5.28 Where the roads forming the approaches to a junction are of equal traffic importance, the highway authority will need to decide which is to be regarded as the major road and mark the others accordingly. At some junctions the road conditions may be such that it would be preferable to regard a road of greater traffic importance as the minor road for the purpose of the GIVE WAY marking. For example, at a square cross road intersection where the East/West route is on a steep gradient and the major traffic route turns from South to East, it may be preferable to mark the approaches from the North and South.

5.29 Unless there are special reasons to the contrary, the marking would not be appropriate in the following circumstances:

(a) On high speed dual carriageway roads where traffic either joins from a slip road (at a grade separated junction) or there s an acceleration splay and no gap in the central reserve. At such sites the normal edge of carriageway marking would be appropriate.

(b) At "Y" junctions where two one-way traffic streams merge at an acute angle.

(c) On the approaches to weaving sections of certain complex road layouts.

5.30 Where traffic from a minor road joins a major road on an acceleration splay at a level intersection with either (a) a dual carriageway road where there is a gap in the central reserve, or (b) a high speed single carriageway road, the length of the transverse GIVE WAY marking should extend from the centre line to the left for a width equal to that of the minor road; the remainder of the acceleration splay should be marked with the normal edge of carriageway marking, (see Fig 5:53).

5.31 On two-way approaches the GIVE WAY transverse marking should always be accompanied by a central longitudinal warning line extending back from the junction in accordance with the standards recommended in Section 6.

**Triangular Give Way Approach Marking** Fig 5:2

5.32 The hollow triangular marking may only be used when a transverse GIVE WAY line is provided. It may or may not be accompanied by a GIVE WAY upright sign. It must not be used elsewhere. The marking should normally be located with its base 2.100m to 2.750m from the transverse marking, but exceptionally this distance may be increased to a maximum of 15m depending on the visibility at the junction, its layout, and the speed of traffic on the minor road. A suitable place to locate it would be with the base of the triangle near the tangent point of the kerbline.

Where triangular markings are used they should be positioned approximately in the centre of the traffic lane. Where the approach to the junction is divided into 2 or more lanes, then, a triangular marking should be provided in each lane.

**Standards of Marking**

5.33 The transverse GIVE WAY marking may be used alone Fig 5:3a or with the triangular approach marking Fig 5:3b. Where used alone it must not be accompanied by an upright GIVE WAY sign.

5.34 A longitudinal warning line extending back the recommended distance from the junction should accompany either arrangement (see Section 6).

5.35 Subject to the exceptions mentioned above, the following standards of signing should be adopted:

(a) The Transverse Marking, Give Way Sign and Triangular Approach Marking Fig 5:3b should be provided: —

100
(150)
(200)

300

600

4000(6000)

2000
(3000)

600

1250

150

300

600

3750

200

2100-2750
(max. 15000)

300

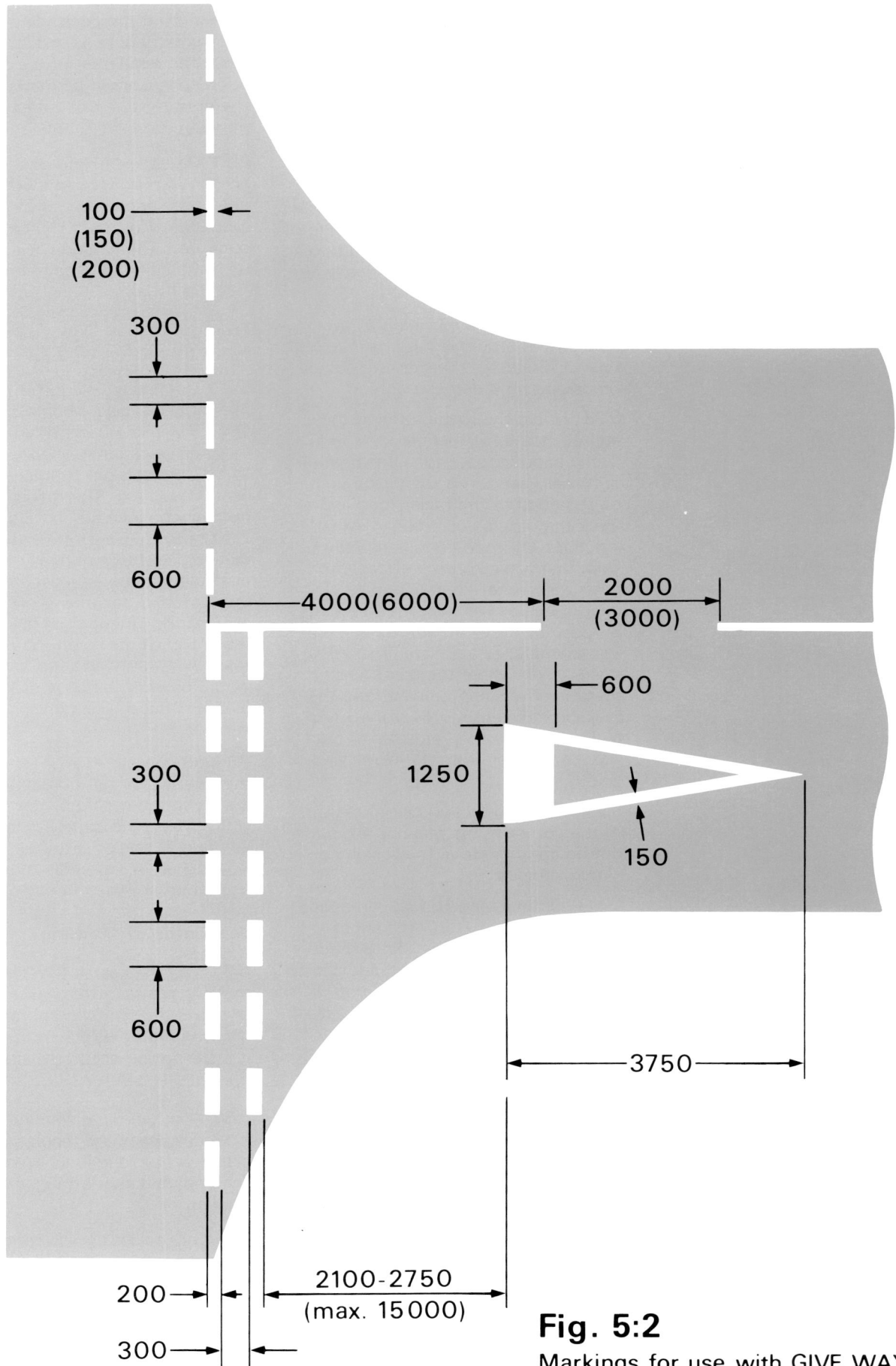

**Fig. 5:2**
Markings for use with GIVE WAY sign

**(Example shown where 1m strip provided)**

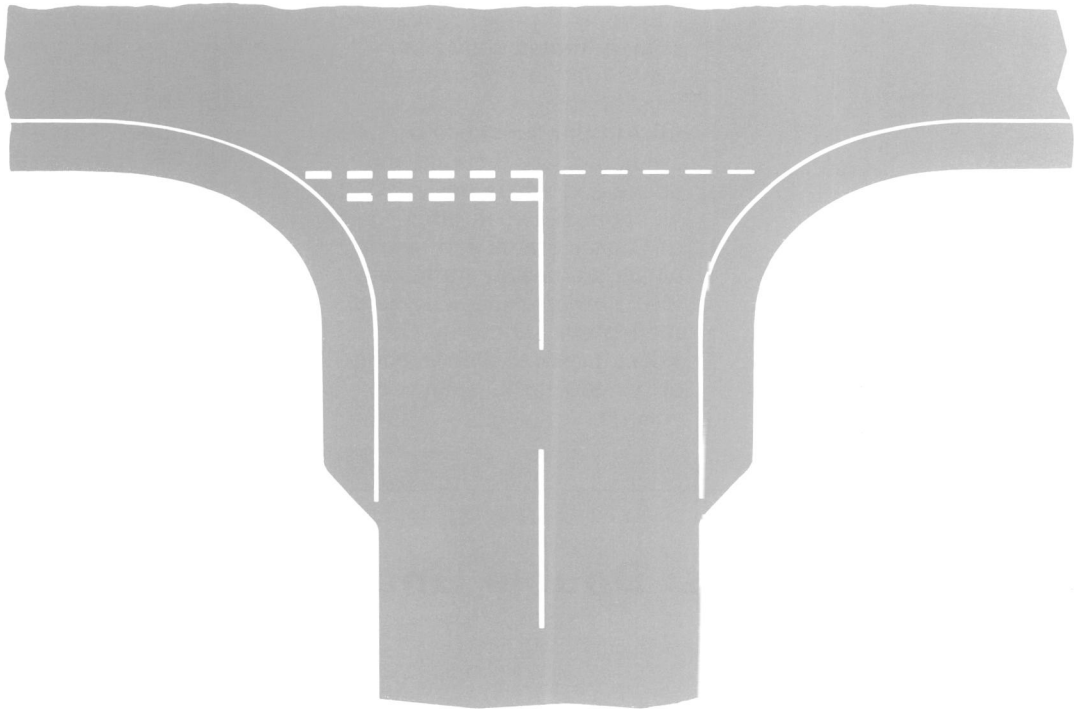

**(a)**

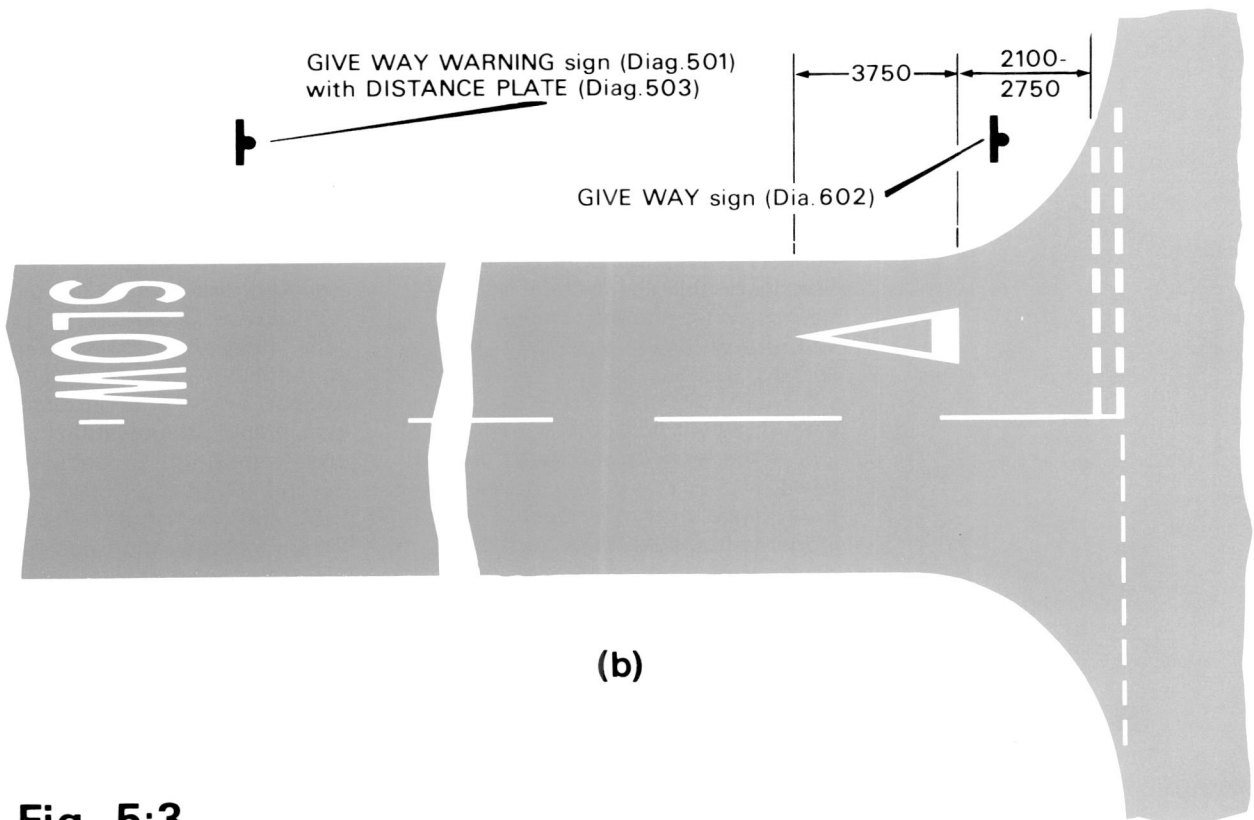

GIVE WAY WARNING sign (Diag.501)
with DISTANCE PLATE (Diag.503)

GIVE WAY sign (Dia.602)

3750   2100-2750

**(b)**

# Fig. 5:3
Alternative layouts GIVE WAY markings

(1) In rural areas at all junctions of public roads with primary routes.

(2) In urban areas generally at junctions of public roads with primary routes unless the minor road is a residential or local street.

(3) At other junctions between roads of Class II status and above and where advisable at junctions between other roads of Class II status and below which are heavily trafficked.

(4) At other junctions where the highway authority considers it desirable on account of danger, traffic speeds or volume.

NOTE: Where the conditions are such that an advance GIVE WAY warning sign (Diag. 501) with plate (Diag. 503) is necessary, the advance sign may be supplemented by the SLOW marking on the carriageway Fig 5:3b.

(b) The Transverse Marking with Triangular Approach Markings Fig 5:2 OR Transverse Markings alone Fig 5:3a should be provided at the junctions of public roads other than those defined in (a).

5.36 The SLOW marking, but not the advance GIVE WAY warning sign, may be used to give advance warning of junctions signed as described in 5.35 (b).

# 5. Longitudinal Markings: Double Line System

5.37 The double line system provides a means of prohibiting overtaking on lengths of road where *visibility* is restricted. The double lines permit each direction of travel to be separately marked according to the lack of visibility in that direction. The standard of visibility justifying the use of these lines and hence the lengths of lines themselves is strictly governed by the speeds of vehicles on the road. Where visibility is just above the minimum standard, but overtaking may nevertheless present danger, or where it is impossible to use the double line system (eg, because of restricted carriageway width) a single warning line is prescribed, see Section 6.

5.38 *It should be borne in mind that where the visibility standards are satisfied, it does not automatically follow that double lines must be laid down;* judgement should be exercised in deciding whether, having regard to the topographical and traffic characteristics of the route, it is reasonable to impose the restrictions or whether the warning type of line should be used instead. Double lines impose arbitrary restrictions on some drivers—for example those who because they are seated higher above the road have a better range of vision—and it is important that the lines should not be used where the appropriate standards are not satisfied.

5.39 Highway authorities should ensure that all newly laid double line markings conform to the criteria set out in the subsequent paragraphs. The emphasis should always be on *not* using double lines except where they are clearly justified on these criteria, both in relation to the length in question and as part of a route as a whole. It is not necessary to obtain formal authorisation for the lines because discretion in deciding where to use double lines, or warning or lane lines instead, is left to highway authorities. However, as contravention of the prohibitory line is a punishable offence and is subject to the "totting-up" procedure (Sections 93 and 101 of the Road Traffic Act 1972 and the Fourth Schedule thereto as amended by the Road Traffic Act 1974) the appropriate Commissioner of Police or Chief Constable should always be consulted wherever it is proposed to lay down new double line markings. Highway authorities should also furnish the appropriate Director (Transport) with copies of plans showing their proposals for any new lengths of double lines so that his officers may have an opportunity to satisfy themselves that the lines are fully justified.

5.40 Double lines should not normally be used in built up areas, because it is unduly restrictive to prevent vehicles stopping in this way. They may, however, be required at certain difficult positions. In this case, the visibility distances for 30 mph (50 kph) should be used for speeds of 30 mph (50 kph) or less. If the 85% ile speed is higher than 30 mph (50 kph) notwithstanding the legal limit, then the appropriate visibility distances should be those for the actual 85% ile speed.

5.41 Methods of determining speed and visibility distances are described in Appendices I and II respectively.

5.42 Double lines consist of a 150mm wide continuous prohibitory line accompanied either by another continuous line or a broken permissive line to provide for the different forward visibilities in opposite directions. The continuous prohibitory line is installed where the visibility on bends or humps is less than the following "prohibitory" criteria, the speed being that which includes 85 per cent of drivers and the visibility distance being measured from an eye-height of 1.05m to a target of the same height above the road level.

## TABLE A:

# Prohibitory Lines

| Marking | Figure No. | Mark (mm) | Gap (mm) | Width (mm) | Stud Spacing (mm) |
|---|---|---|---|---|---|
| Prohibitory | 5:4 | CONTINUOUS | CONTINUOUS | 150 (100 minimum) | 4000 |
| Permissive broken | 5:4 | 1000 | 5000 | 150 (100 Minimum) | |

USE

These lines comprise the Double Line System. The continuous prohibitory line is always accompanied either by another continuous line or a permissive broken line. The two lines are spaced 175mm (90mm minimum) apart with reflecting road studs between them.

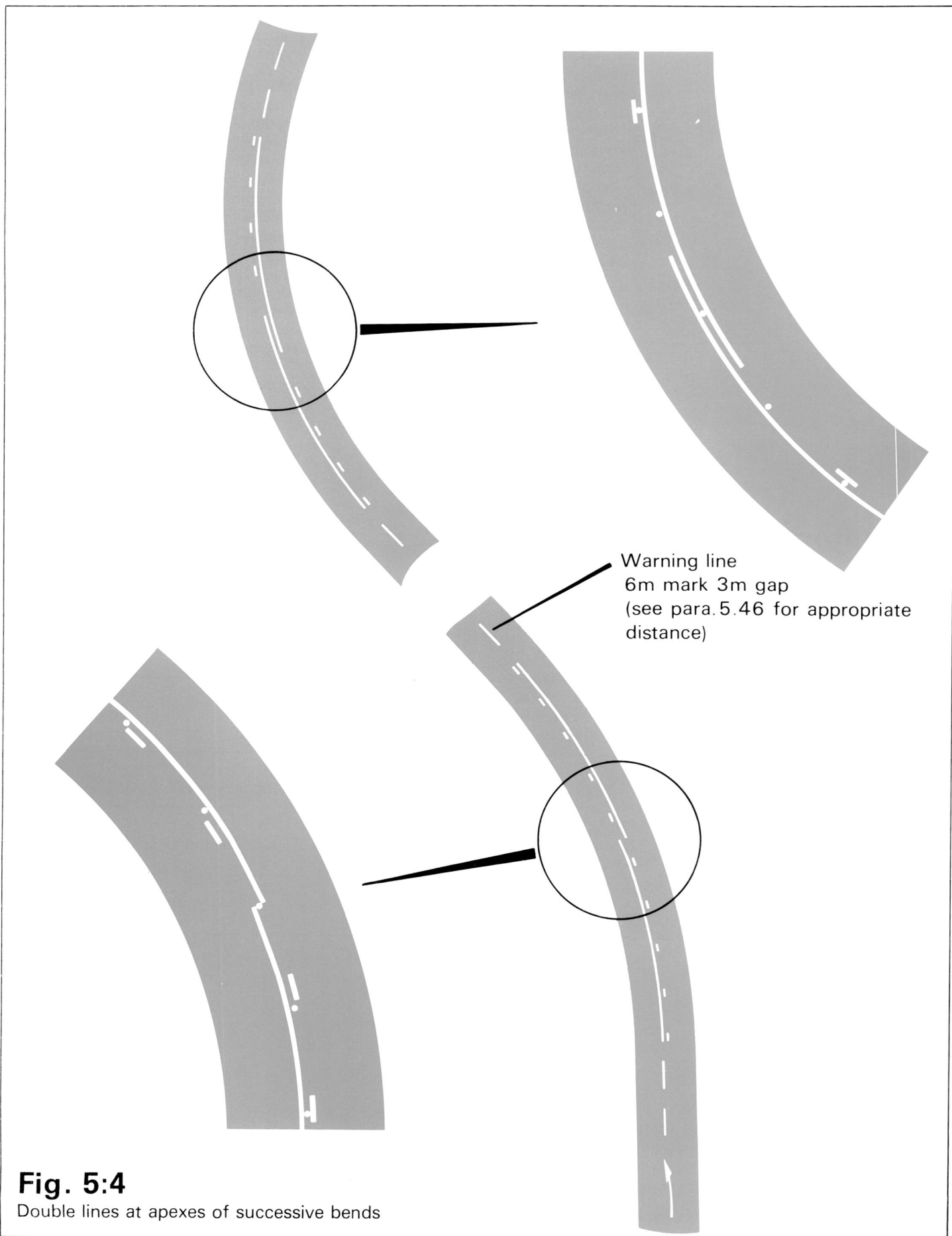

Warning line
6m mark 3m gap
(see para.5.46 for appropriate
distance)

## Fig. 5:4

Double lines at apexes of successive bends

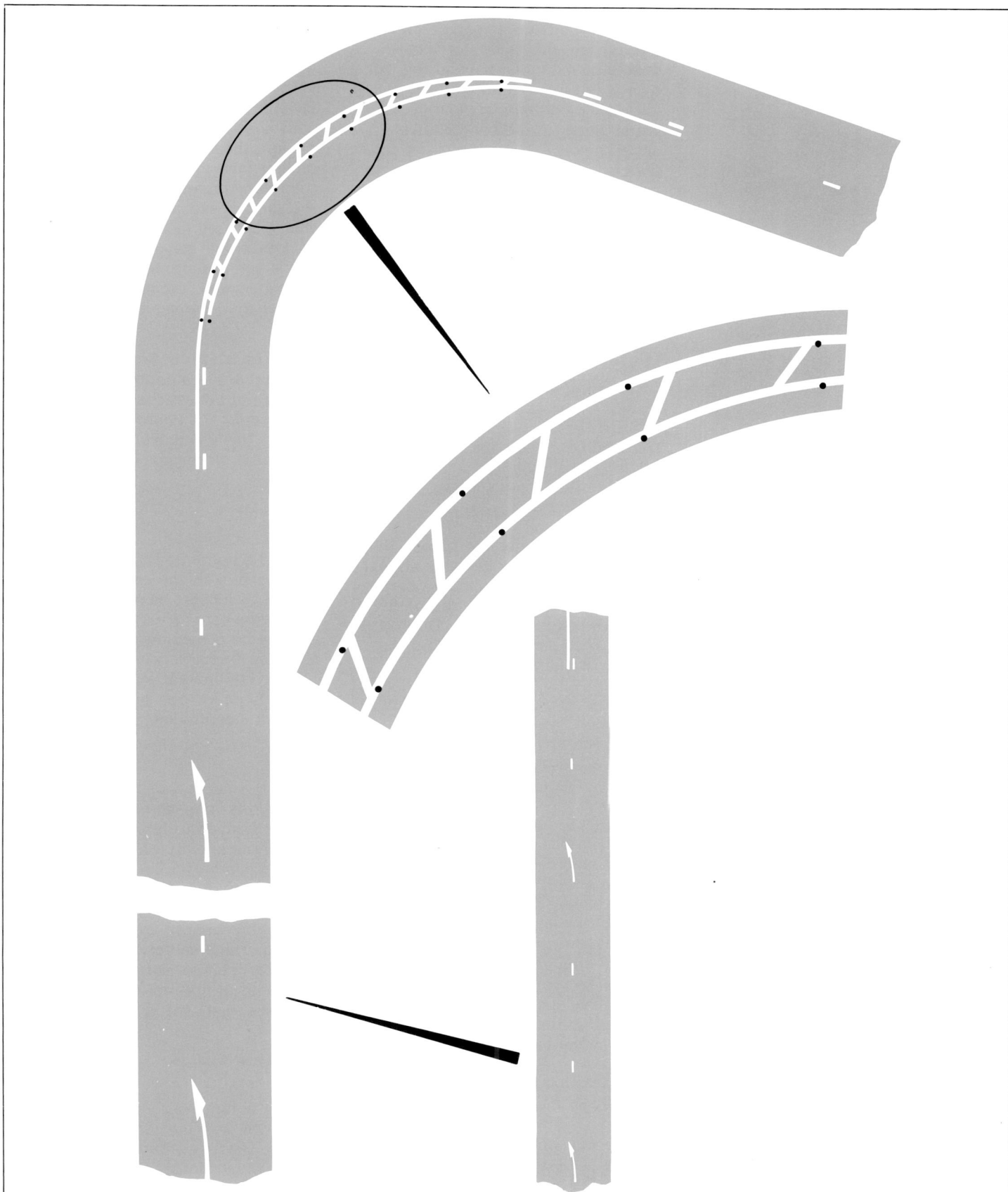

# Fig. 5:5
Double lines and hatched markings on sharp bends

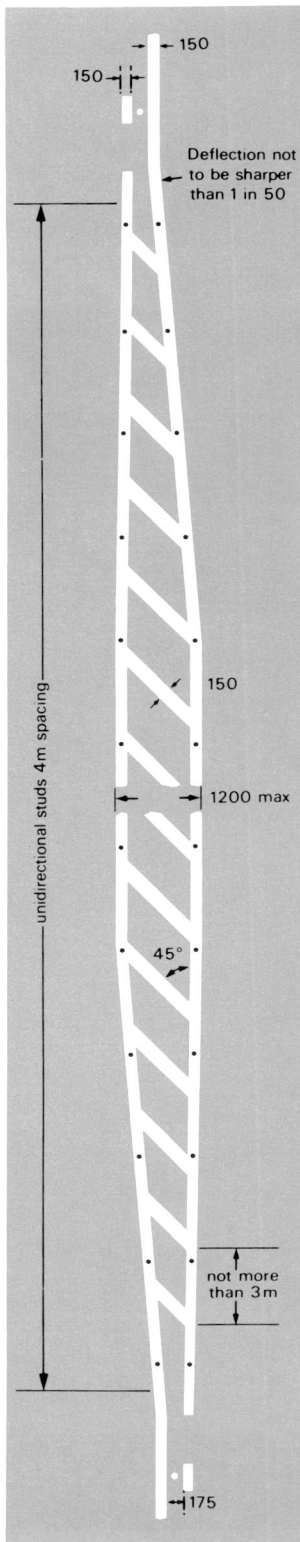

**Fig. 5:6**
Double lines and hatched markings at humps or dips

As conditions are different on the inside of the bend as compared with the outside, the prohibitory line should be extended beyond the exit from a left-hand bend until the warning visibility criteria (see para 5.61) are attained. In the comparatively rare cases, however, where the exit continuous line would otherwise extend beyond the entrance continuous line for traffic in the other direction, it should be stopped level with the entrance line, as this is less likely to confuse drivers.

| 85%ile SPEED (kph) | 60 | 70 | 85 | 100 | 120 |
|---|---|---|---|---|---|
| 85%ile SPEED (mph) | 37 | 43 | 53 | 62 | 74 |
| VISIBILITY DISTANCE (metres) | 90 | 105 | 125 | 155 | 185 |

(measured between points on the centre of the carriageway)
NOTE: For intermediate speeds, the appropriate visibility distance should be taken as the higher figure between the steps shown. eg. With an 85%ile speed of 65kph (40 mph), Double White Lines are justified when the visibility is 105m or less.

5.43 The second line in a double line installation, where the visibility is better than the "prohibitory" criterion, is a broken line with a 1m mark 150mm wide and a 5m gap (Table A).

5.44 All double line sections must be marked with a single row of bi-directional white reflecting studs spaced at 4m intervals. These must be laid between the lines, except that when the lines are splayed to form a hatched area uni-directional studs must be laid symmetrically in each longitudinal line at 4m intervals arranged so that only the studs nearest the driver reflect back.

5.45 All double lines must be laid in reflectorised material.

*The Relationship of Solid Lines at the Apexes of Successive Bends and of Humps Figs 5:4 and 5:5.*

5.46 According to the physical characteristics of a bend or hump, the solid lines for traffic in opposing directions can either overlap or have a gap between them. If they overlap,

there will be a section of double continuous line in the middle. If, however, they do not meet and there is a gap, Fig 5:4, which is less than the visibility distance for the appropriate 85% ile speed (see para 5.42) the two solid lines should be extended to meet in the centre of the gap; if it is greater than this distance but less than the warning visibility distance for the same speed, a single warning line should be used to join the two sections of double line: beyond that the lane line is appropriate, as at any other site where the visibility distance is greater than the warning criterion.

5.47 The length of a broken line element within a double line system should not be less than the visibility distance for the appropriate 85% ile speed. This will prevent overtaking where the distance is insufficient.

**Bends**

5.48 The continuous line of a continuous/broken line combination should be located along the centre line of the carriageway, giving the driver who is restricted by it his full share of the carriageway width. Double continuous lines should normally be located symmetrically about the centre line of the carriageway.

5.49 On sharp bends where double continuous lines are required, they can be splayed to form a sort of central island with a maximum overall outside width of 1.2m, provided there is ample room on either side to enable vehicles to negotiate the bend reasonably without crossing the lines Fig 5:5. The area between the lines must be hatched with inclined 150mm wide lines at not more than 3m spacings as shown in Fig 5:6

**Humps and Dips**

5.50 A hump should be treated in the same way as a horizontal bend as regards visibility criteria and line markings, except that where double continuous lines are required, the lines should be opened out at an inclination not exceeding 1 in 50 as they approach the point of minimum visibility (often not the highest point) to attain a maximum overall outside width of 1.2m. The lines which

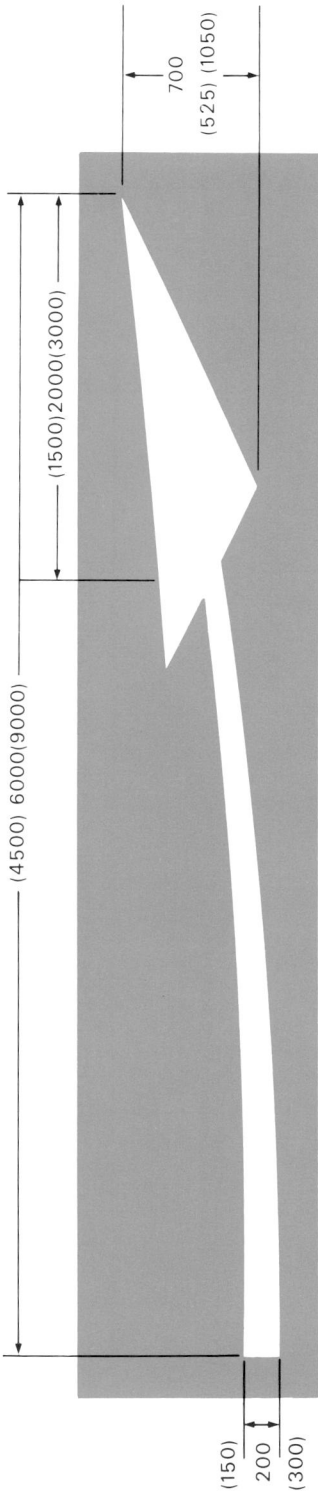

**Fig. 5:7**
Warning Arrow

Used on the approach to double white lines. May be used on the approaches to diagonally hatched areas where advanced warning is advisable.

enclose these widened areas must be continuous, and the area between the lines must be hatched with the marking shown in Fig 5:6. The humps either side of a dip should be treated individually.

### Road Widths

5.51 Having regard to the road width required by public service and commercial vehicles, particularly on sharp bends, double line markings should not normally be used where the carriageway is less than 6.1m in width; the 100mm warning line should be used instead.

### Warning Arrows Fig. 5:7

5.52 Drivers must be given warning of their approach to any arrangement of double lines by at least one arrow on the carriageway directing them towards the left-hand side of the road. Approach warning arrows are usually positioned in the centre of the carriageway Fig 5:7(a) but where they are required because of a length of broken line within a double white line system, the arrows should be positioned approximately 1m to the right of the continuous line so as to avoid breaking the double white line pattern, Fig 5:7(b).

5.53 General Direction 42 of the Traffic Signs Regulations and General Directions 1981 requires the provision of one arrow per approach, but where space permits two arrows should normally be provided. Where a driver's forward visibility on the road surface is limited, as on a gradual hump, three arrows may be required to give adequate forewarning. When arrows are to be laid in the centre of a two-lane road, the marks in the centre line (either lane or warning) should be removed and each arrow laid in the centre of the gap so formed, Fig 5:5.

5.54 The first arrow should normally be spaced 1 second of travel time back from the beginning of the double line, and the second arrow another 2 seconds of travel time back from the first. If this second one is not visible to drivers 6 seconds travel time away, ie 9 seconds from the double line, then a third arrow should be installed 3 seconds travel time back from the second arrow. For practical purposes the arrow spacings in feet are 1½, 3

and 4½ times the speed in miles per hour Fig 5:7(a).

5.55 The use of *off-set* double lines on alternate sections of three lane roads to facilitate overtaking in the centre lane is not recommended. Carriageways of 10m or more in width should be marked with a centre of carriageway marking in accordance with Table C.

### Exceptional uses of Double Lines

5.56 Two exceptional circumstances are given below where double lines may be used, even though the conditions do not meet the recommended visibility criteria. Proposals for their use in these circumstances should be referred to the Director (Transport) before the lines are laid.

(a) On 10m carriageways on long hills Fig 5:8. Off-set double white lines comprising a continuous and a broken line should be laid so as to reserve 2 lanes to ascending traffic and enable faster moving vehicles to overtake slower ones in safety. Provided the visibility distance for drivers descending a hill does not fall below the criteria for the prohibitory line, the broken line component should be on the side of the single lane so that a vehicle descending a hill can overtake a slower vehicle provided the driver can see that it is safe to do so.

(b) At Level Crossings
See section 9 for details.

### Inclined Lines at Refuges

5.57 Double lines should not be splayed where they meet a refuge. Both lines on the double combination should be inclined, keeping them parallel so that the nearest line (whether continuous or broken) joins the nearside of the refuge Fig 5:12a). Lines should not be continued alongside the refuge. The degree of inclination should be the same as for warning lines, as set out in paragraph 5.70.

### Changes of Pattern

5.58 A change of pattern, ie a change from a double continuous to a continuous/broken line combination should not be made when it results in a length of continuous/broken line of less than the appropriate visibility distance shown in the table in paragraph 5.42.

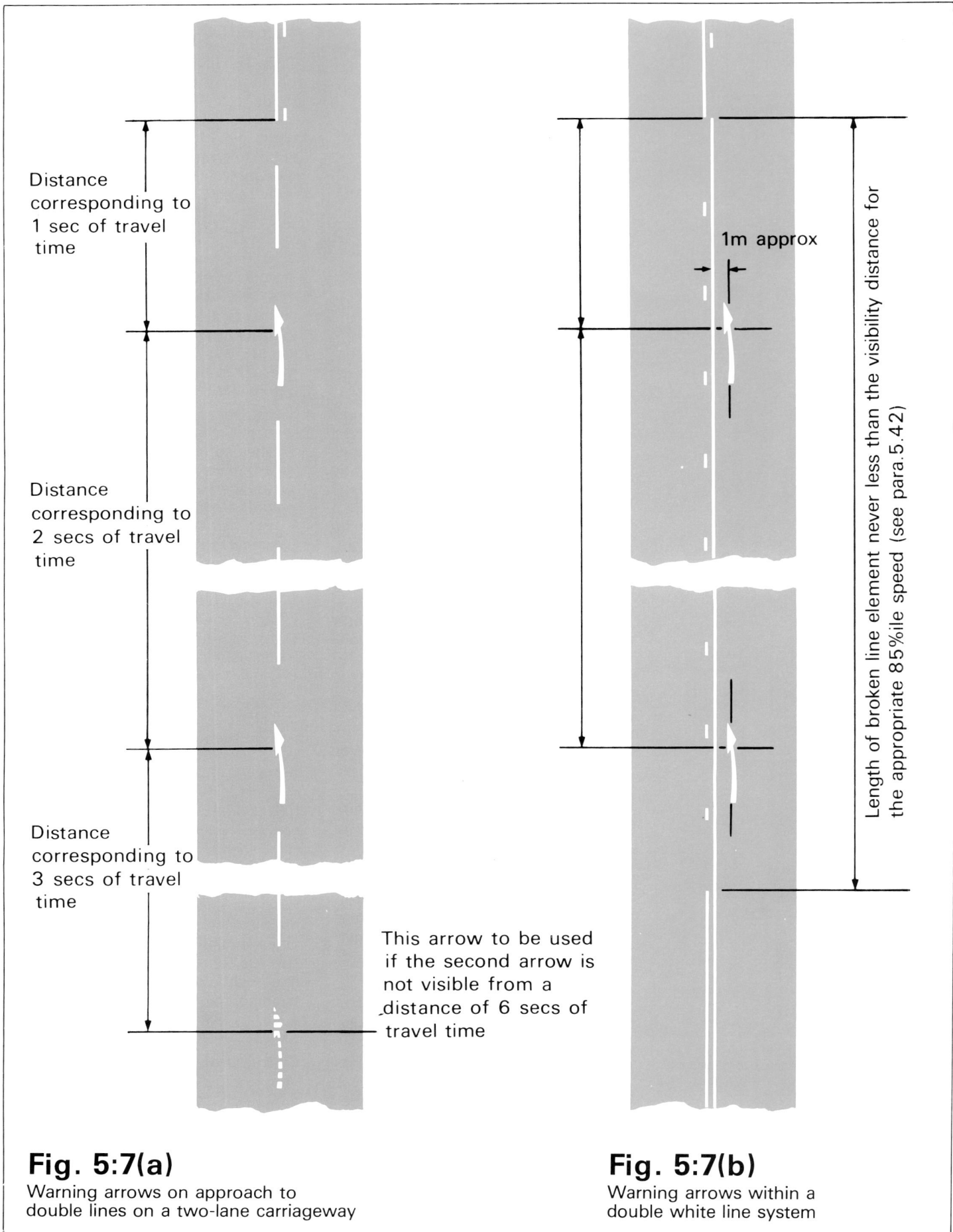

Distance corresponding to 1 sec of travel time

Distance corresponding to 2 secs of travel time

Distance corresponding to 3 secs of travel time

This arrow to be used if the second arrow is not visible from a distance of 6 secs of travel time

1m approx

Length of broken line element never less than the visibility distance for the appropriate 85%ile speed (see para.5.42)

## Fig. 5:7(a)
Warning arrows on approach to double lines on a two-lane carriageway

## Fig. 5:7(b)
Warning arrows within a double white line system

Plan of road and markings approaching hill

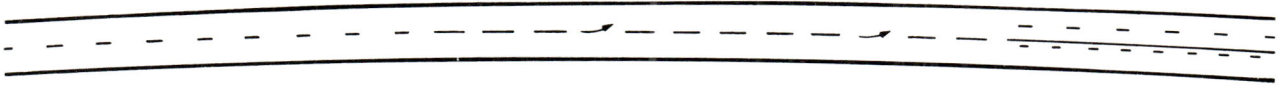

## Fig. 5:8
Double lines on a long 3-lane hill, dividing carriageway into two up and one down lane

### Road Junctions

5.59 It should be borne in mind that the Regulations contain an exemption permitting vehicles to cross the continuous line to obtain access to any other road or private access joining the length of road along which the line is placed and a gap in the line is not therefore necessary.

### Practical Points

(i) A double line must not be used at sites where, for example, a busy road is narrow and has a bad accident record, when in fact visibility is above the criteria justifying the prohibitory lines. Such provisions may well lead to disregard for the prohibitory markings.

(ii) Double lines should not be used at points where the visibility may be below the criteria, but where a few seconds beforehand the driver had a view of the now obscured section; such conditions may arise on winding hills with small clumps of trees or bushes.

5.60 Not allocated.

# 6. Longitudinal Markings: Warning Lines Fig. 5:9

5.61 These are broken lines with the marks twice as long as the gaps. They are installed at bends and humps where the visibility is greater than the 'prohibitory' criteria in Section 5, but less than the following 'warning' criteria:

| 85%ile SPEED (kph) | 60 | 70 | 85 | 100 | 120 |
|---|---|---|---|---|---|
| 85%ile SPEED (mph) | 37 | 43 | 53 | 62 | 74 |

VISIBILITY
DISTANCE  145  175  205  245  290
(measured between points on the centre of the carriageway)
NOTE: For intermediate speeds, the appropriate visibility distance should be taken as the higher figure between the steps shown. eg With an 85% ile speed of 65kph (40mph), Warning Lines are justified when the visibility is 175m or less.

5.62 Warning lines should also be used where it is necessary to give warning of the presence of a road junction and to mark the approach to central refuges, except where these are within a double line section. The overall length of these approach warning lines will vary between approximately 20 and 80 metres depending on vehicle speeds and whether the site is 'urban' or 'rural'.

5.63 Warning lines are always single; they should never be used as part of a double line installation.

5.64 Two patterns of warning line are prescribed, each having two widths.

The combined length of one mark and one gap is known as the module. There are two standard modules, depending on the speed of the road.

| Pattern | Speed Limit | Module |
|---|---|---|
| 'URBAN' | 40mph (60kph) or less | 6m |
| 'RURAL' | Over 40mph (60kph) or unrestricted | 9m |

5.65 Details of the lines and circumstances in which they should be used are set out in Table B.

5.66 The number of marks at junctions quoted in the table are a minimum. They should be extended wherever justified by the road or traffic conditions.

5.67 Lines used for dividing the carriageway into lanes at the immediate approaches to junctions, including signal control junctions should follow these patterns. The detailed arrangements for marking signal controlled junctions are described in Section 13.

5.68 Where warning lines are used on single carriageway roads to separate opposing flows of traffic, they should normally be laid in the geometric centre of the carriageway. At bends the lane width should never be less than on the immediate approaches.

5.69 Where it is necessary to change the position of lines in relation to the width of the road, the deflection should be smooth and made at an inclination not greater than 1:20.

## TABLE B

# Warning Lines

*'URBAN'— Restricted to 40mph (60Kph) or less (6,000mm module)*

| Fig No. | Mark (mm) | Gap (mm) | Width (mm) | Stud Spacing (mm) (if used) | Use | Minimum No of marks | |
|---|---|---|---|---|---|---|---|
| | | | | | | Speed Limit mph (Kph) | |
| | | | | | | 40 (60) | 30 (50) |
| 5:9 | 4,000 | 2,000 | 100 | 6,000 | 1. Central warning line on two lane roads. | 7 | 5 |
| | | | | | 2. Lane line on immediate approaches to signal controlled junctions | 7 | 5 |
| 5:9 | 4,000 | 2,000 | 150 | 6,000 | 1. Central warning line on roads of three lane width | 7 | 5 |
| | | | | | 2. Central warning line on four or six lane roads on immediate approaches to signal controlled junctions | 10 | 7 |

*'RURAL'— Speed limit over 40mph (60Kph) or unrestricted (9,000mm module)*

| Fig No. | Mark (mm) | Gap (mm) | Width (mm) | Stud Spacing (mm) (if used) | Use | Minimum No of Marks |
|---|---|---|---|---|---|---|
| 5:9 | 6,000 | 3,000 | 100 | 9,000 | 1. Central warning line on two lane roads. | 7 |
| | | | | | 2. Lane line on immediate approaches to signal controlled junctions | 7 |
| 5:9 | 6,000 | 3,000 | 150 | 9,000 | 1. Central warning line on roads of three lane width | 7 |
| | | | | | 2. Central warning line on four or six lane roads on immediate approaches to signal controlled junctions | 10 |

### Inclined Lines at Refuges

5.70 A warning line approaching a refuge should be inclined for its full length (see TABLE B for minimum number of marks), terminating in a position 300mm from the nearside edge of the refuge Fig 5:12b. For a wide refuge or a central reserve the inclined warning line should be extended as necessary so as to attain an inclination not greater than 1:20 for 30mph (50Kph) or 1:50 for 60mph (100Kph) with proportionate inclinations for intermediate speeds. See section 15 for further advice.

### Other Inclined Lines

5.71 The inclined line steering traffic from the middle lane of three to the nearside of two should be of the warning type, and should comprise not less than 5 marks in the inclined portion in urban areas and 7 marks in rural areas. Sharp changes of direction, which may sometimes arise where the inclined line joins a warning or prohibitory line on a bend, should be eased out in accordance with the inclinations given in the previous section.

### Changes in Pattern

5.72 A change of pattern involving a warning line, ie a change from a double to warning line or warning to lane line, should not be made when it results in a length of warning line less than 90m. Judgment must be exercised in deciding whether to omit short sections of warning lines or whether to extend them to the minimum length quoted.

### Road Junctions

5.73 On straight sections of road, warning lines would normally be appropriate when the average traffic volumes from the side road exceed about 100 vehicles per hour. In these circumstances the lane marking should be changed to a warning line right through the junction extending for a distance varying between approximately 20 and 80m on each approach (see Table B), depending on vehicle speeds and whether the road is in a rural or urban area.

5.74 On bends which are marked with warning or prohibitory lines the above criteria for approach markings at junctions will not apply. Warning line on the minor road approaches should not be carried across the major road.

# 7. Longitudinal Markings: Lane and Centre of Carriageway Lines   Figs 5:10 and 5:11

5.75 The benefits to be gained from the use of lane and centre of carriageway lines in both urban and rural areas cannot be stressed too strongly. By guiding and confining traffic to its correct lane, the lines have an important bearing on safety, besides ensuring that all the available carriageway space is used to its maximum capacity. Wide-spread use of the lines should be made wherever possible and highway authorities are strongly recommended to introduce lane and centre lines where appropriate on roads in their areas which are not now so marked.

5.76 Details of the lines and the circumstances in which they should be used are set out in Table C.

5.77 The advice given in paragraphs 5.68 and 5.69 relating to the lateral location of warning lines is equally applicable for lane lines.

5.78 to 5.80 Not allocated.

TABLE C

# Lane and Centre of Carriageway Lines

*'URBAN'—Restricted to 40mph (60Kph) or less (6,000mm module)*

| Marking | Fig No. | Mark (mm) | Gap (mm) | Width (mm) | Stud Spacing (mm) (if used) | Use |
|---|---|---|---|---|---|---|
| Lane lines | 5:10 | 1,000 | 5,000 | 100 | 12,000 | Division of carriageway into traffic lanes. |
| Centre of carriageway lines (See also Table B) | 5:11 | 1,000 | 5,000 | 100 | 12,000 | Two lane carriageway 6,000mm or more in width. |
| | 5:11 | 1,000 | 5,000 | 100 | Not Required | Two lane 'town centre'(Note 2) |
| | 5:11 | 3,000 | 3,000 | 100 (150) | 6,000 | Four or more lanes or 10m or more in width |

*'RURAL'—Speed limit over 40mph (60Kph) or unrestricted (9,000mm module)*

| Marking | Fig No. | Mark (mm) | Gap (mm) | Width (mm) | Stud Spacing (mm) (if used) | Use |
|---|---|---|---|---|---|---|
| Lane lines | 5:10 | 2,000 | 7,000 | 100 | 18,000 (Note 1) | Division of carriageway into traffic lanes. |
| | 5:10 | 2,000 | 7,000 | 100 | 18,000 | Division of carriageway into traffic lanes on dual carriageway roads with a design speed of 120Kph or over, or when 85 percentile speed is 100Kph or over. |
| | 5:10 | 2,000 | 7,000 | 100 | 18,000 | Division of carriageway into lanes on motorways. |
| Centre of carriageway lines (See also Table B) | 5:10 | 2,000 | 7,000 | 100 | 18,000 (Note 1) | Two lane carriageways 5,500mm or more in width. |
| | 5:11 | 3,000 | 3,000 | 150 | 6,000 | Four or more lanes or 10m or more in width. |

NOTE 1. On bends, the radius of curvature of which is less than 450m the stud spacing should be reduced to 9m. On roads subject to fog and mist and on two-way roads carrying heavy traffic volumes where there is a severe dazzle problem the stud spacing may be reduced to 9m.

NOTE 2. For use as centre line in busy urban streets where parked cars and waiting vehicles confine moving vehicles to one lane in each direction.

Urban

4m

2m

stud spacing
6m if used

100 (150)

Rural

6m

3m

9m

100 (150)

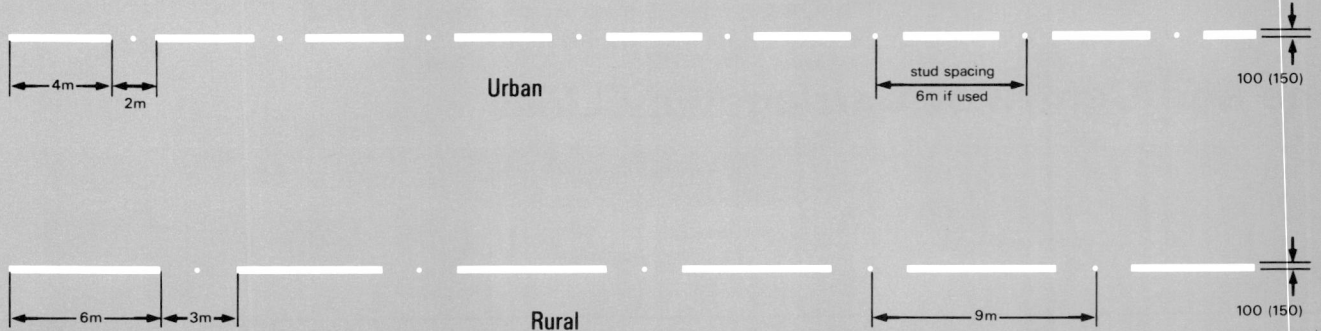

## Fig. 5:9 (Diag. 1004)
Warning markings (Table B)

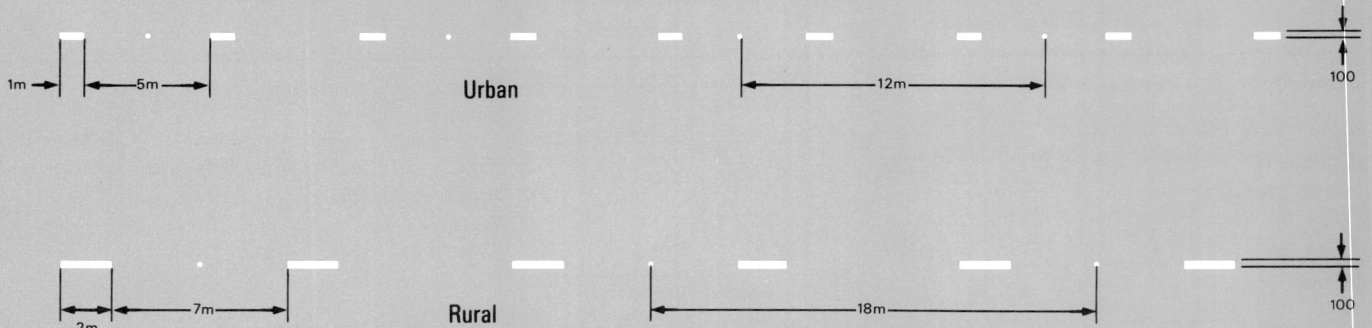

Urban

1m

5m

12m

100

Rural

2m

7m

18m

100

## Fig. 5:10 (Diag. 1005)
Lane markings (Table C)

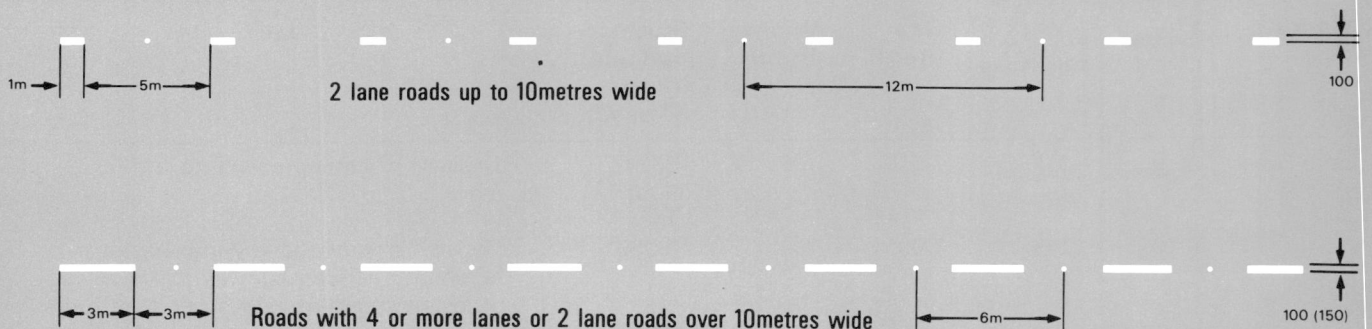

1m

5m

2 lane roads up to 10metres wide

12m

100

3m

3m

Roads with 4 or more lanes or 2 lane roads over 10metres wide

6m

100 (150)

## Fig. 5:11 (Diag. 1007)
Centre of carriageway markings (Table C)

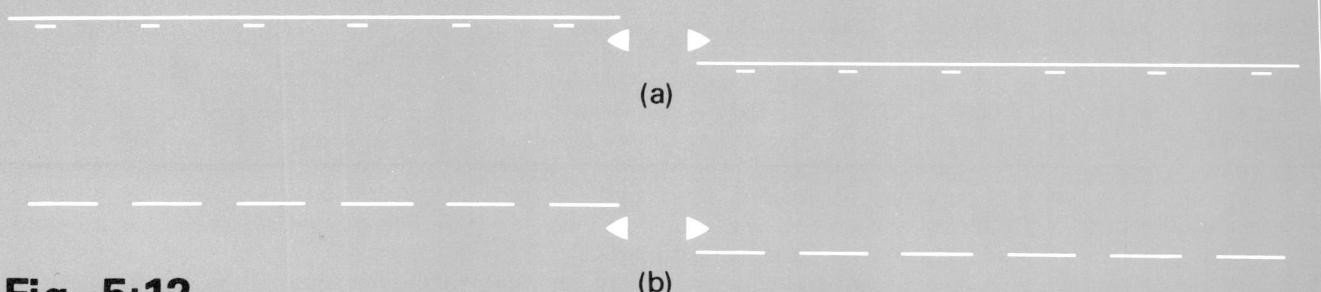

(a)

(b)

## Fig. 5:12
Inclined lines at refuges

# 8.  Longitudinal Markings: Edge of Carriageway Lines

5.81 Three forms of marking are prescribed (see Table D and Fig 5:13).

**TYPE A** (Figs 5.42, 5.44, 5.45, 5.51 and 5.53) is used to indicate the edge of the carriageway where this may be in doubt, eg at wide mouthed junctions in conjunction with Give Way lines at acceleration and deceleration splays at gaps in central reservations and at lay-bys.

5.82 The prescribed pattern consists of a broken line comprising alternate marks and gaps, each 1m long.

5.83 Three widths of line are used according to the following criteria:

|  | WIDTH |
|---|---|
| 'URBAN' roads, subject to a speed limit of 40mph (60kph) or less | — 100mm |
| 'RURAL' roads, subject to a speed limit of over 40mph (60kph) | — 150mm |
| 'RURAL' roads, unrestricted | — 200mm |
| 'MOTORWAYS', across the mouths of slip roads | — 200mm |

The 100mm wide line should normally be used to mark the continuation of the carriageway at lay-bys. However, when hard shoulders or hard strips are provided and 150mm wide edge lines are used, the line across lay-bys should also be 150mm wide.

5.84 The markings should be reflectorised when laid on unlit roads. Alternatively, they may be provided with uni-directional reflecting road studs showing green on the driver's nearside, with the stud spacing not exceeding 18m. (See Table D.)

5.85 On motorways where this marking is laid across acceleration/ deceleration tapers at standard junctions, uni-directional green reflecting road studs are used at 8m centres.

5.86 **TYPE B** (Fig 5:2) extends the transverse GIVE WAY and STOP line markings at junctions. Where the minor road carries two-way traffic, the transverse GIVE WAY and STOP markings may in appropriate cases be extended across the entry half width of the minor road by means of a *single* broken line having the same mark/gap pattern as the GIVE WAY marking (600mm mark 300mm gap). The normal width of the line is 100mm but the wider 150mm or 200mm line may be used where the continuity of the edge of carriageway of the major road needs special emphasis.
The line should comprise at least 5 marks, ie it is only appropriate when the half width to the tangent point of

the major road kerbline exceeds about 4.5m.

5.87 The marking should only be used where it is desired to preserve the continuity of the edge of the carriageway of the major road, and then only in conjunction with the GIVE WAY and STOP transverse marking at junctions. It must not be used to delineate the edges of the carriageway in other situations, eg at lay-bys or at acceleration and deceleration splays, for which the Type A edge of carriageway marking is appropriate.

5.88 **TYPE C** (Fig 5:13). These markings are intended for wide-spread use to delineate the edge of the carriageway on unlit rural roads without clearly defined raised kerbs.

5.89 Trials have shown that the markings have merit as a safety measure despite the fact that their efficiency may sometimes be impaired by dirt because of their location near the edge of the carriageway.

5.90 They are strongly recommended on *all* unlit rural roads without raised kerbs, but priority should be given to those roads which are generally sinuous in character and which carry large volumes of traffic.

5.91 The prescribed markings, which should always be reflectorised or incorporate crushed calcined flint, consist of either:
    C(i) a broken line comprising a 1m (1.5m) mark and a 3.5m (3m) gap;
or  C(ii) and (iii) a single continuous line.

5.92 Both C(i) and (ii) are 100mm wide and, except where there are flush kerbs, are laid in the carriageway with the inside edge of the line approximately 225mm from the nearside edge of the carriageway. Where flush kerbs are provided, the edge linings should be superimposed on the kerb. The markings should not be carried across the mouths of side roads, acceleration or deceleration splays or lay-bys.

5.93 The markings should not normally be used where the carriageway is less than 6.1m in width or where the lane width between an edge line and any centre line is less than 2.75m.

5.94 The alternative broken line dimensions given in para 5.91 above, are intended for use at sites where silt

## TABLE D

# Edge of Carriageway Lines

| Markings | Fig No | Mark (mm) | Gap (mm) | Width (mm) | Stud Spacing (mm) (if used) | Use |
|---|---|---|---|---|---|---|
| (TYPE A) | 5:13 | 1,000 | 1,000 | 100 (150) (200) | 18,000 (max) 2,000 (min) | To indicate the edge of the carriageway at wide mouth junctions and laybys. The intermediate line (150) is appropriate on roads with a speed limit of over 40mph (60kph). The wider line is appropriate on unrestricted all purpose roads. |
| | 5:13 | 1,000 | 1,000 | 250 | | Bus Lanes |
| | 5:13 | 1,000 | 1,000 | 200 (300) | 8,000 | To indicate the edge of the carriageway on motorways at slip road junctions. The wider line is not recommended for future use. |
| (TYPE B) | 5:13 | 600 | 300 | 100 150 200 | | These lines extend the STOP and GIVE WAY lines across the entry half of the minor road at a junction. |
| (TYPE C(i)) | 5:13 | 1,000 | 3,500 | 100 | 18,000 | In rural areas on unlighted primary routes without kerbs and on other heavily trafficked roads which are poorly aligned and where the after dark conditions call for special delineation of the edge of the carriageway. |
| (TYPE C(ii)) | 5:13 | Continuous | | 100 | 9,000 | At particularly hazardous situations e.g. sudden changes of carriageway width and on approaches to bends. |
| (TYPE C(iii)) | 5:13 | Continuous | | 200 (150) (300) | 18,000 | Edgelining on motorways. The narrower line is used on all purpose dual and single carriageway roads where hard shoulders or hard strips are provided. The wider line is not recommended for future use. |

**TYPE A** (Diag.1010)

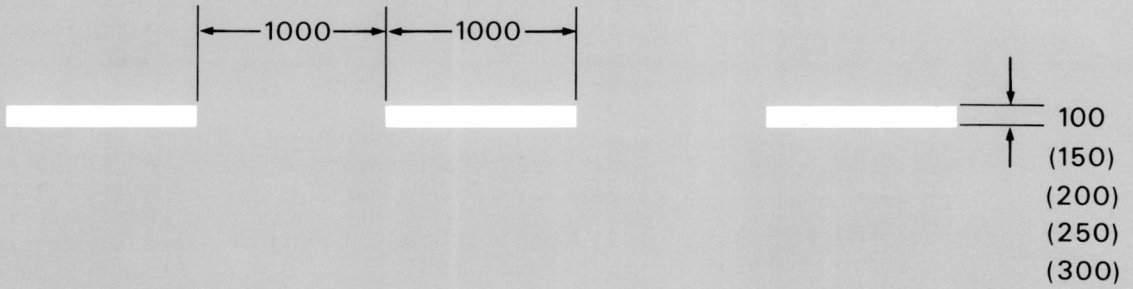

|←— 1000 —→|←— 1000 —→|

100
(150)
(200)
(250)
(300)

**TYPE B** (Diag.1009)

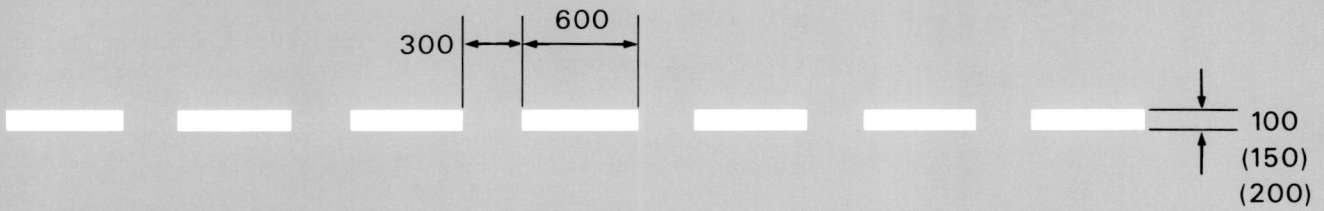

300 |←— 600 —→|

100
(150)
(200)

**TYPE C** (Diags.1011, 1012 & 1012.1)

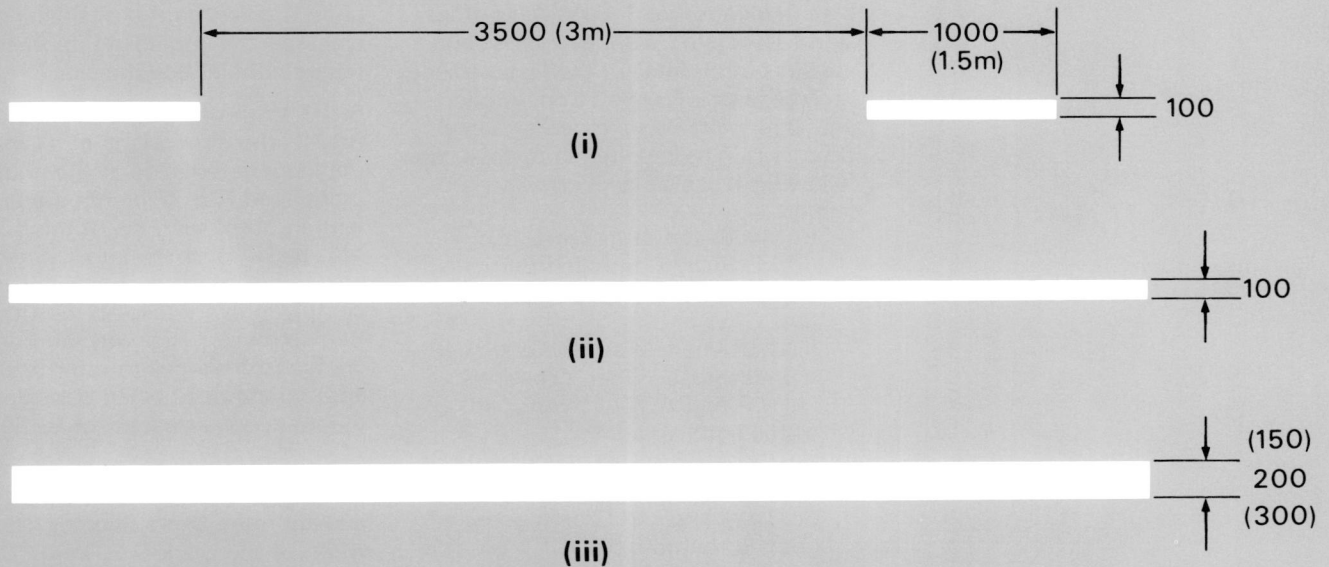

|←——————— 3500 (3m) ———————→||←— 1000 —→|
(1.5m)

100

**(i)**

100

**(ii)**

(150)
200
(300)

**(iii)**

## Fig. 5:13
Edge of carriageway lines

is frequently washed from the verge onto the carriageway edge or where ponding occurs and the markings tend to become obscured.

5.95 The following are examples of the situations where the more emphatic continuous line, Type C(ii), marking might be appropriate:

(i) Where the demarcation between the carriageway and the verge is particularly bad;

(ii) Along lengths which are prone to fog and mist;

(iii) On heavily trafficked two and three-lane roads where headlamp dazzle is severe;

(iv) At sudden changes of carriageway width;

(v) On the approaches to narrow bridges;

(vi) On the approaches to bends indicated by bend warning signs.

5.96 Where used, the length of the continuous line should correspond with that of any prohibitory or warning lines in the centre of the carriageway where these exist, and should of course continue through the hazard. Elsewhere the broken line is used.

5.97 Edge lines are also recommended for use along the right-hand carriageway edge of unlit dual carriageway roads. In these circumstances the line, which will normally be broken, should be laid approximately 225mm away from, and parallel with, the central reserve.

5.98 Where, because of the importance or nature of the road, additional emphasis is required, reflecting road studs may be used. (See Table D).

5.99 Type C(iii) continuous edge markings used on motorways and all purpose roads with hard shoulders or hardstrips. (See Table D).

5.100 not allocated.

# 9. Markings at Level Crossings

5.101 The arrangement of carriageway markings, road studs, and other signs associated with level crossings are set out in detail in the Department of Transport's Railway Construction and Operation Requirements — Level Crossings. The requirements cover the following types of level crossing protection:
(i) Manually Controlled Gates
(ii) Manually Controlled Barriers (MCB) (includes those supervised by CCTV)
(iii) Automatic Half Barriers (AHB)
(iv) Automatic Open Crossings (AOCR and AOCL) (with road traffic light signals)
(v) Open Crossings (OC) (without road traffic light signals)
(vi) User Worked Crossings with gates or barriers (UWC)
(vii) Miniature Red/Green Warning Lights (MWL)

5.102 These Requirements give comprehensive information on the layout and operation of the Crossing and on any road traffic light signs, road markings and rail and road signs required. The location of the road signs approaching a crossing follow

standard highway practice and guidance is given on the positioning of signs on the immediate approaches where conflict could arise.

5.103 With one exception (see para 5.104), the dimensions of all road markings referred to in the above-mentioned Requirements are dealt with in other sections of this Chapter but, because of the importance of ensuring that all level crossings comply in every respect with the Requirements, Highway Authorities are advised always to refer to the appropriate ones when considering the markings at a level crossing.

5.104 Pedestrian GIVE WAY line. This consists of a single broken line with a 500mm mark and a 250mm gap. The width of the mark is 200mm. This transverse marking across the offside of the carriageway and any footway is used to indicate where pedestrians should wait at level crossings when the red lights begin to flash. It is provided at Automatic Half Barrier and Automatic Open Level Crossings (AHB AOCR and AOCL).

5.105 to 5.110 not allocated.

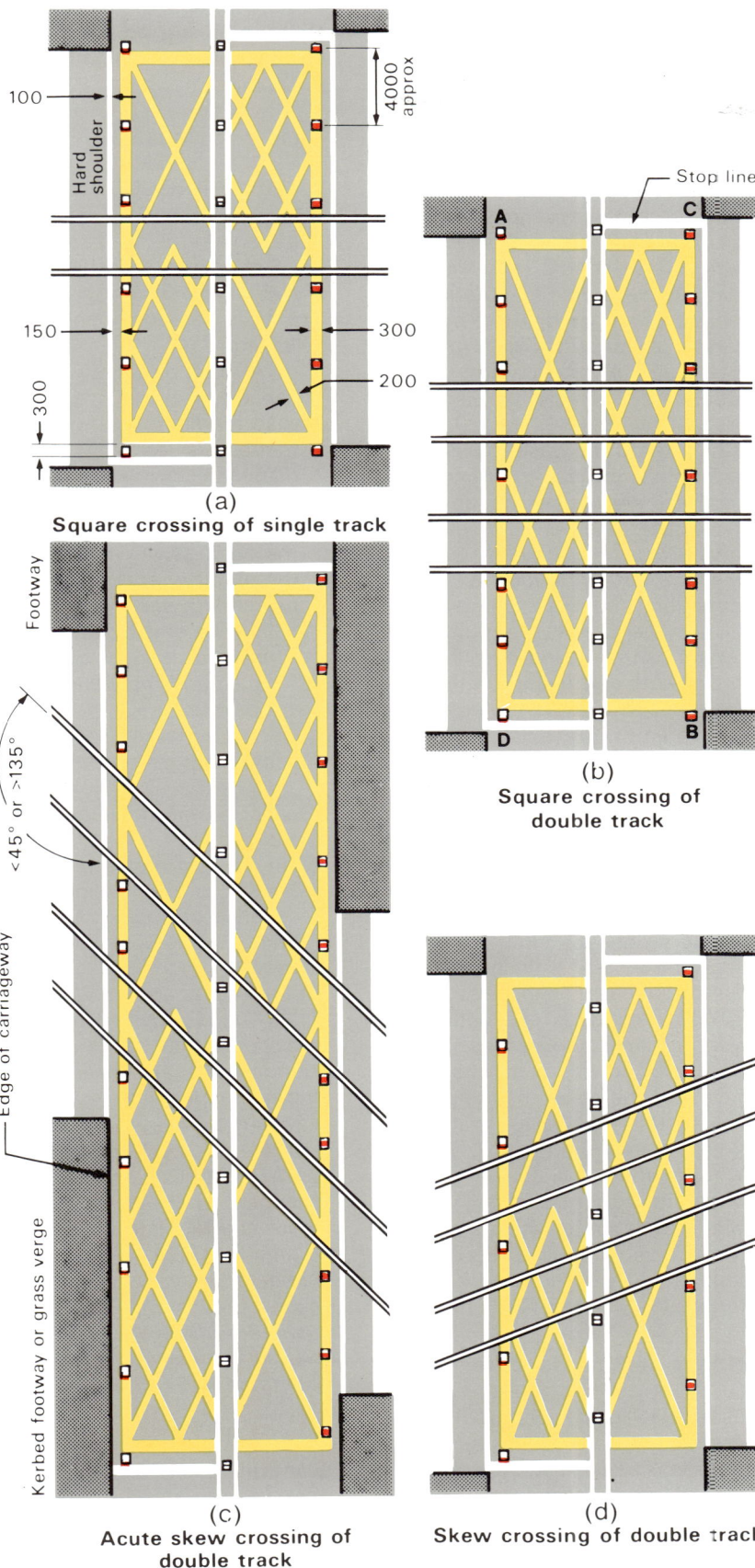

(a)
**Square crossing of single track**

(b)
**Square crossing of double track**

(c)
**Acute skew crossing of double track**

(d)
**Skew crossing of double track**

NOTES

Bi-directional reflecting road studs laid at 4 metre spacing incorporated with longitudinal centre markings shall be all white. To prevent damage to trailing coupling linkages, studs should not be laid between the running rails.

At automatic half barrier level crossings, uni-directional reflecting road studs at the edge of the carriageway shall show red to the drivers left-hand side and shall be set on the carriageway 150–300mm from the edge. Studs shall be at 4 metre spacing on the left hand side of the road on both approaches to the crossing. They should commence at the beginning of the broken/continuous double white lines and extend to the commencement of the crossing area.* Studs shall also be laid at 4 metre spacing at both edges of the crossing area.* ANY STUD LAID WITHIN 2 METRES OF A RUNNING RAIL MUST BE OF PLASTIC CONSTRUCTION.

*The crossing area is that position of the road contained between the lowered barriers and lines joining the barrier tips to their respective duplicate primary signals.

KEY

Uni-directional red reflecting road stud.

Bi-directional white reflecting road stud.

# Fig. 5:14 (Diag. 159)
Arrangement of box and other road markings with automatic half-barriers (see para. 5.149(i))

# 10. Roundabouts

## Introduction

5.111 The general rule governing the behaviour of traffic at roundabouts is given in the Highway Code. The rule advises drivers that when entering a roundabout they should Give Way to any traffic on their immediate right unless road markings indicate otherwise, but should keep moving if the way is clear. Implementation of this basic rule is carried out by the provision of *advisory* Give Way lines across the entry of each arm of the roundabout.

5.112 Of the three basic types of roundabouts, the most common in general use are the normal and mini roundabouts. They are defined as follows: —

(i) Normal Roundabout: a roundabout having a one-way circulatory carriageway, around a kerbed central island over 4 metres in diameter and usually with flared approaches to allow multiple vehicle entry. For signing purposes, the normal roundabout is subdivided into two categories, i.e. those with a central island over 8 metres in diameter and those with a central island between 4 metres and 8 metres in diameter.

(ii) Mini Roundabout: a roundabout having a one-way circulatory carriageway around a flush or slightly raised circular marking less than 4 metres in diameter and with or without flared approaches, (see para 5.287 for requirements on the height of the raised markings).

The third basic type of roundabout is the double roundabout. This type of roundabout will consist of either two normal roundabouts or two mini roundabouts which are either contiguous (see Fig 5:15(a)) or, connected by a central link road or kerbed island, (see Fig 5:15(b)).

## Markings at Roundabouts

5.113 NORMAL ROUNDABOUTS. Where the central island is 8 metres or more in diameter, the prescribed advisory Give Way marking consists of a single broken line comprising a one metre mark and a one metre gap. The width of the mark is 200mm.

Where the central island is between 4 metres and 8 metres in diameter, the prescribed advisory Give Way marking consists of a single broken line comprising 700mm marks with 300mm gaps. The width of the mark is 500mm.

5.114 Not allocated.

5.115 MINI ROUNDABOUTS Fig 5:16. The prescribed advisory Give Way marking is the same as that used at normal roundabouts between 4 metres and 8 metres in diameter but must be accompanied by the following:

(i) A flush or slightly raised, (but capable of being over-run) circular road marking not more than 4 metres nor less than 1 metre in diameter.

(ii) Three white road arrow markings arranged symmetrically on the carriageway in the centre of the gyratory area. Two sizes are prescribed, see Fig 5:16(c).

(a) The smaller (3,025mm) is used for circular central islands up to and including 2,500mm in diameter.

(b) The larger, (4,450mm) is for use with circular central islands more than 2,500mm in diameter up to and including 4,000mm in diameter.

(iii) Upright regulatory signs Fig 5:16(b), on each approach at a distance of approximately 1.5 metres back from the Give Way line.

At mini roundabouts where no deflection is provided and it is considered that traffic entering the roundabout may, because of its approach speed, disregard the standard *advisory* Give Way line, the *mandatory* Give Way sign should be used Fig 5:16(a), and should be mounted on the same post and above the regulatory sign mentioned in para 5.115(iii). Where used, the *mandatory* Give Way sign must always be accompanied by a *mandatory* Give Way marking and triangular approach marking as illustrated in Fig 5:2.

## General

5.116 *At all roundabouts,* the appropriate prescribed Give Way line should be laid at each entry and should connect the central deflection line or traffic deflection island to the nearside kerb approximately following the line of the inscribed circle in order to maintain visibility from each approach lane Fig 5:17(a).

(a) Contiguous double roundabout

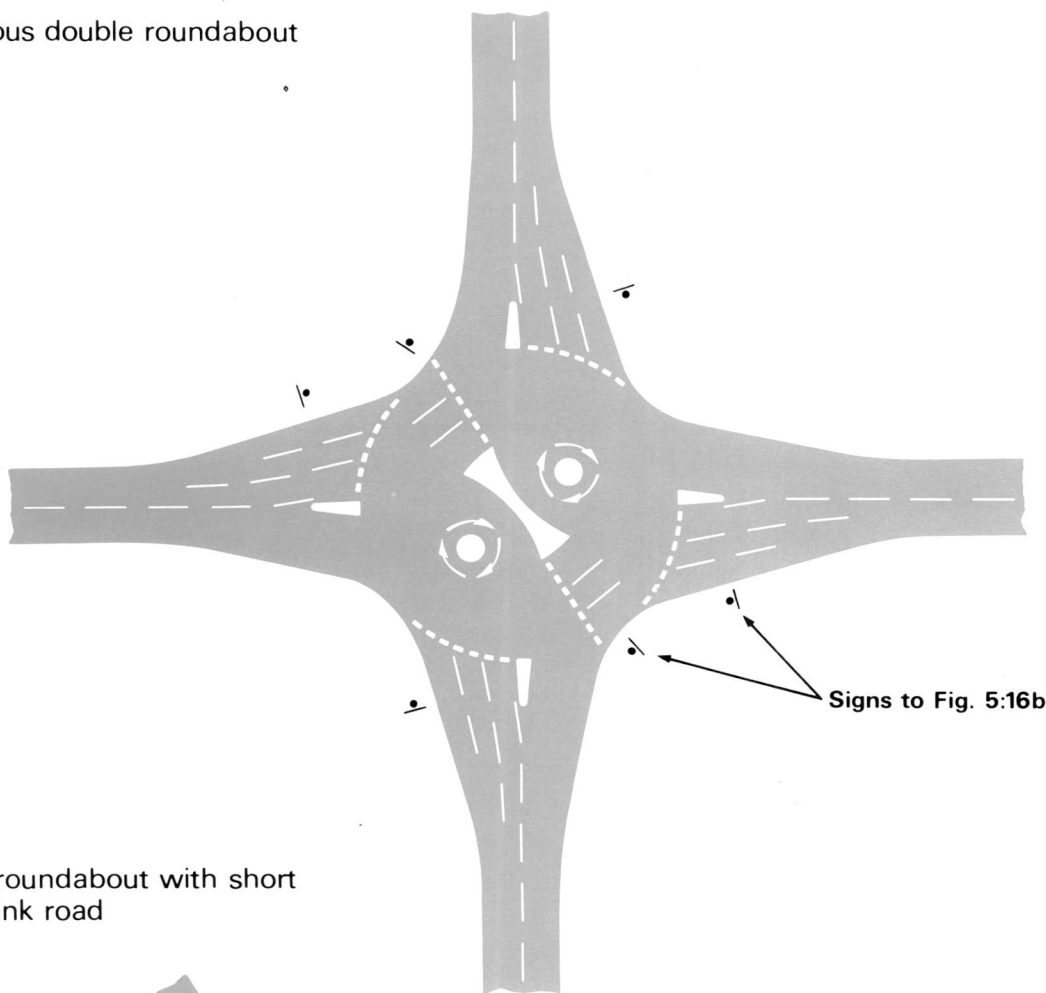

Signs to Fig. 5:16b

(b) Double roundabout with short central link road

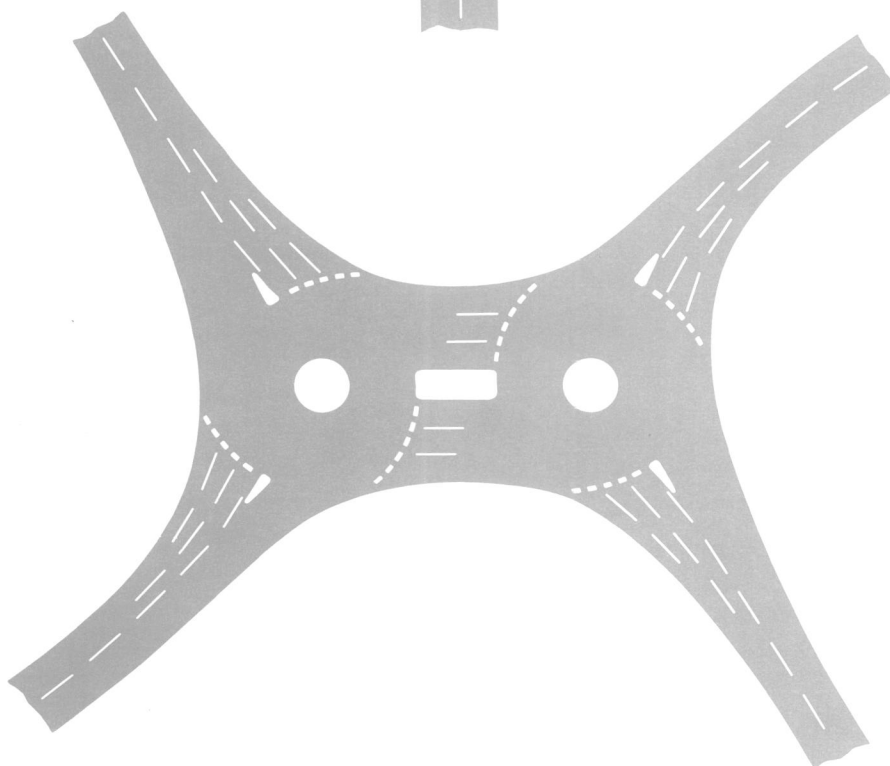

## Fig. 5:15
**Examples of double roundabout layouts**

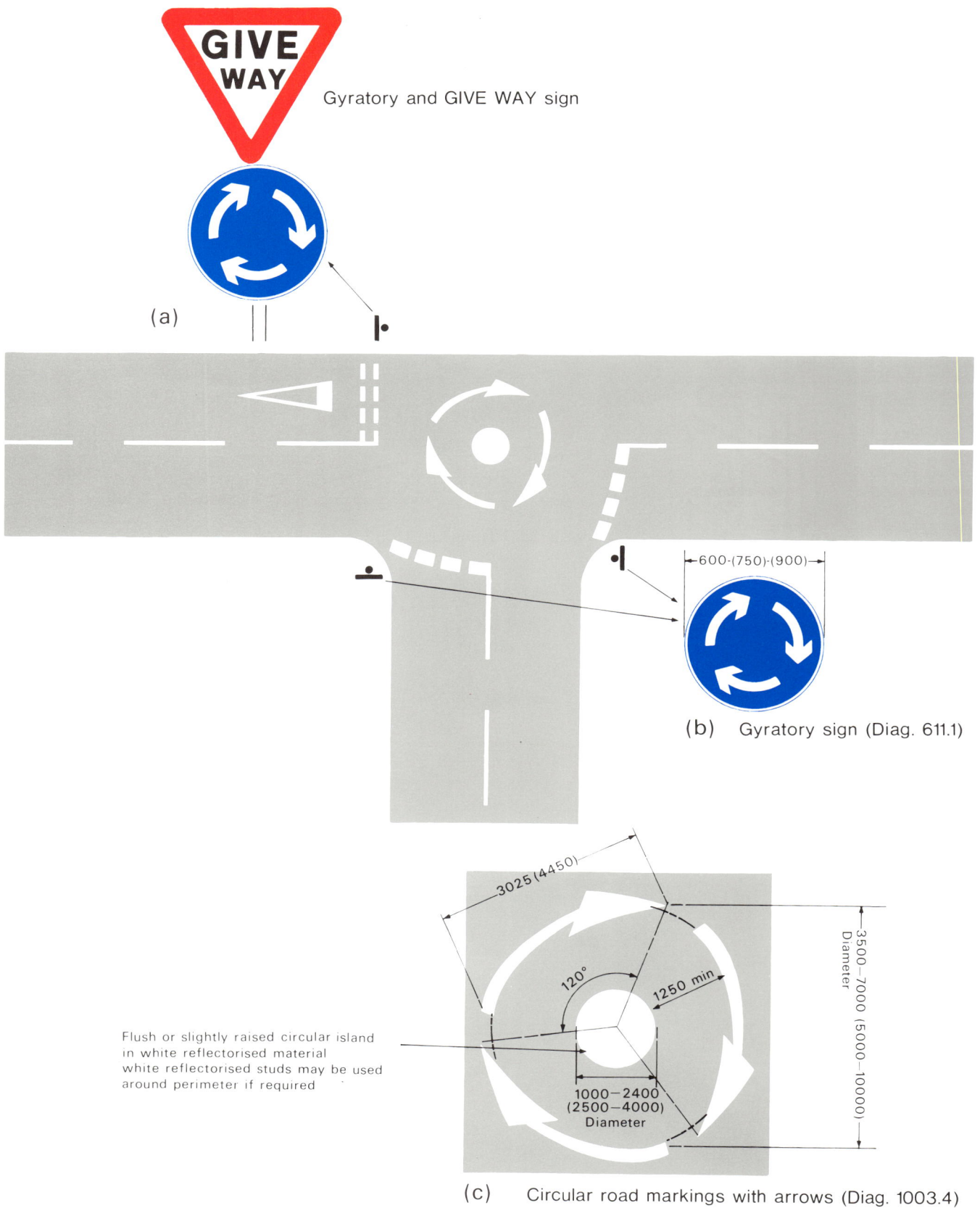

Gyratory and GIVE WAY sign

(a)

(b) Gyratory sign (Diag. 611.1)

←600·(750)·(900)→

3025(4450)

120°

1250 min

3500–7000 (5000–10000) Diameter

Flush or slightly raised circular island in white reflectorised material white reflectorised studs may be used around perimeter if required

1000–2400 (2500–4000) Diameter

(c) Circular road markings with arrows (Diag. 1003.4)

# Fig. 5:16
Arrangement of markings and signs at mini-roundabouts

(a) By central island and central deflection lane

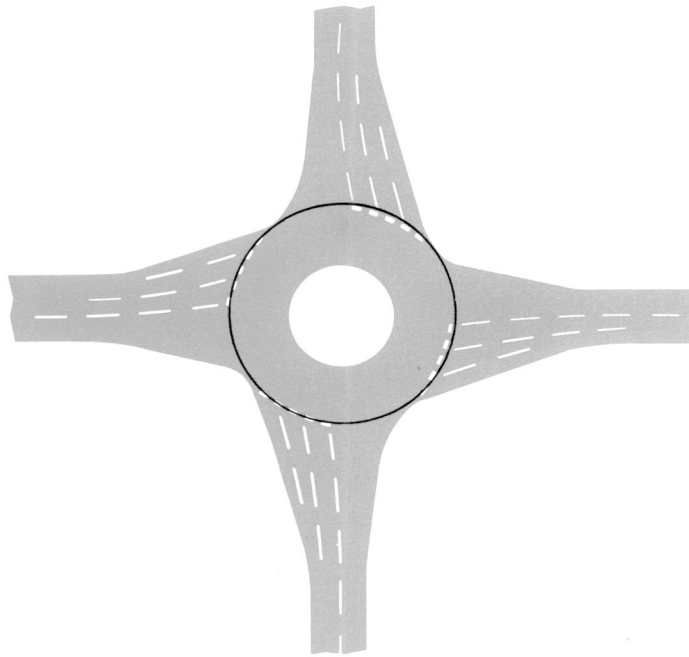

(b) By hatched islands

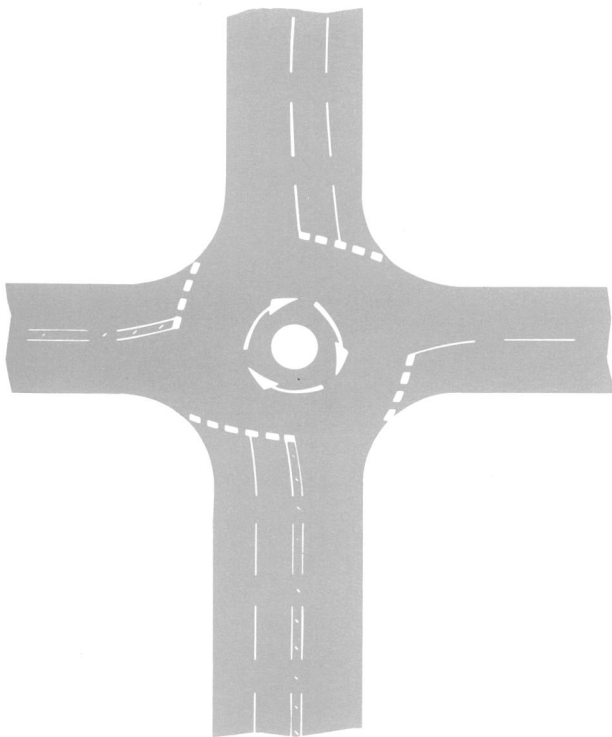

(c) By raised deflection islands

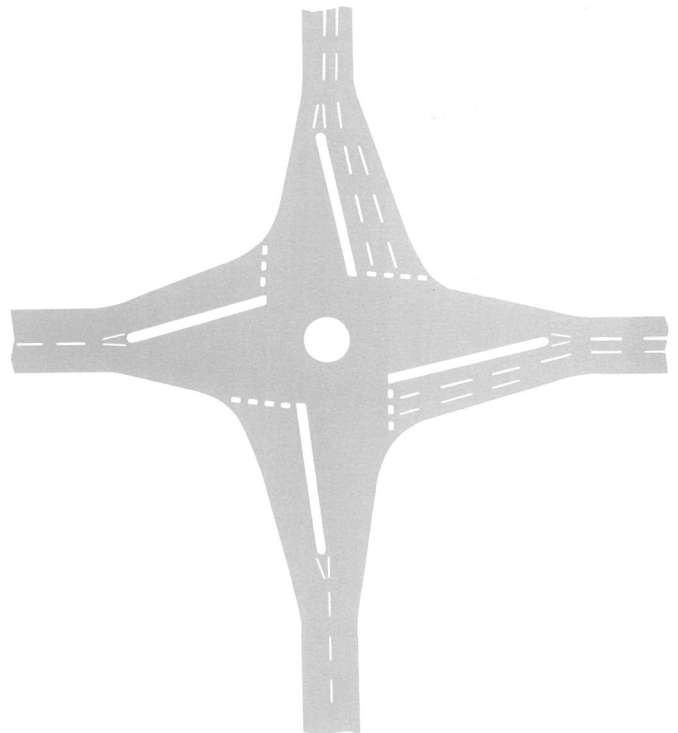

**Fig. 5:17**

Road markings used at roundabouts to provide path deflection

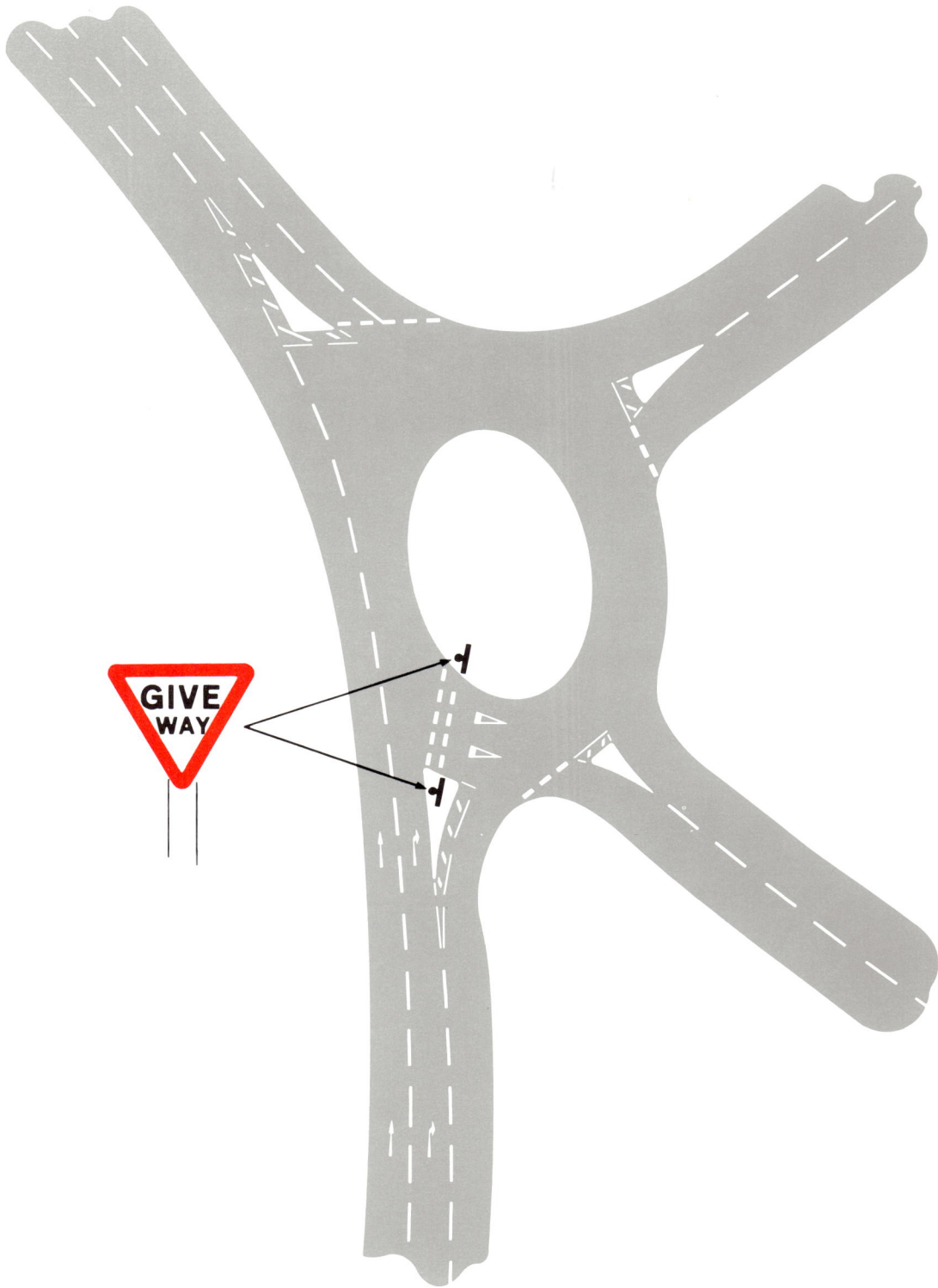

**Fig. 5:18**
Roundabout with GIVE WAY signs within circulatory area

5.117 It is important to provide a specified amount of vehicular deflection through the roundabout as laid down in the Departments' current guidelines on roundabout design. Where raised traffic deflection *islands* are provided to achieve such deflection Fig 5:17(c) the vertical surfaces may be painted in alternate black and white bands 300mm in length to improve their conspicuity. The white bands should be reflectorised with ballotini.

5.118 At sites where an existing junction is being converted to a mini roundabout, full deflection may not be necessary because of low approach speeds, or indeed practical because of site restrictions. Nevertheless, as much of the specified deflection as possible should be the aim and this may be achieved by the provision of hatched markings contained within two broken lines supplemented with white reflecting road studs. It may be advantageous both to increase deflection and encourage maximum use of the entry width to incline such markings initially to the right and then to the left of the centre line.

5.119 Lane markings on the approaches should consist of 4 metre marks each 100mm wide with 2 metre gaps. No other arrow markings or lane markings should be provided on roundabout approaches.

5.120 On rare occasions, at some roundabouts, it is sometimes expedient to give traffic from one arm of a roundabout priority over traffic in the actual roundabout circulation. This usually arises due to an unusual or asymmetrical layout or, the existence of a predominant flow. Layouts of this kind are not recommended where the roundabout appears conventional as viewed by approaching traffic, because they operate contrary to the basic rule and can therefore be confusing and dangerous, particularly to motorists negotiating the roundabout for the first time. This problem can often be dealt with by traffic signal control on one or more of the approaches to the roundabout.

5.121 However, where traffic signals are inappropriate, the layout shown in Fig 5:18 may be used. *Mandatory* double Give Way lines with triangular approach markings as illustrated in Fig 5:2 must be laid within the circulatory area of the roundabout immediately in advance of the particular entry arm that carries the traffic being given priority. The Give Way markings must in addition be reinforced by the provision of two upright Give Way signs, one at each end of the Give Way lines, i.e. one sign on the central island and one on the nearside kerb Fig 5:18.

5.122 to 5.124 not allocated.

# 11. Lines Indicating Waiting, and Loading/Unloading Restrictions

5.125 These are dealt with in Chapter 3—Regulatory Signs—in the Section dealing with Waiting Restriction and Clearway signs. Details of materials and the application of these markings is given in Sections 16 and 17 of this Chapter.

5.126 to 5.129 not allocated.

# 12. Worded Markings, Parking Bays, Bus Stops, Bus Lanes, Yellow Box Markings and Cycle Lanes

**Fig. 5:19** (Diag. 1025)
BUS STOP markings

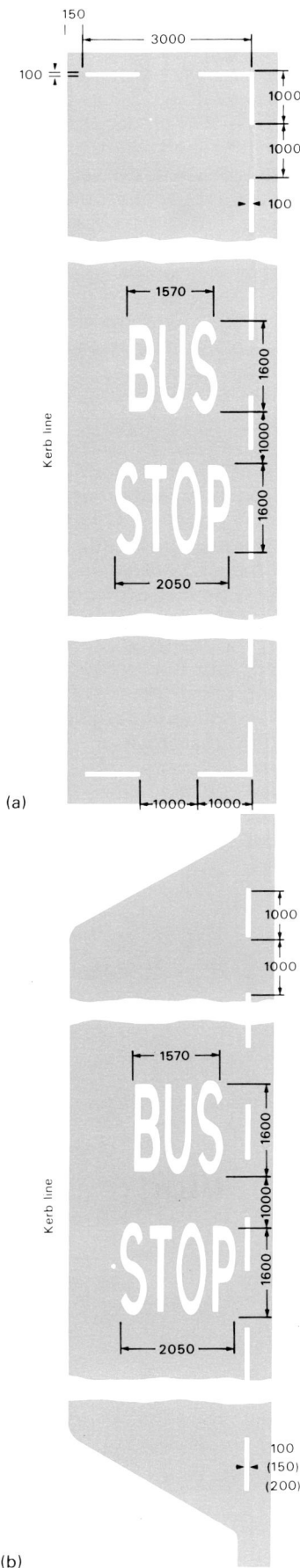

(a)

(b)

## Worded and Box Markings

5.130 Various worded markings are prescribed (see Appendix III). Some augment kerbside signs, others indicate areas of the carriageway intended for a particular function (eg Bus Stop), for classes of vehicle (eg Ambulances), or to be kept clear (eg School Keep Clear). The markings are either white or yellow in colour.

### Stop Fig. 5:1

5.131 This marking must be used to supplement a STOP sign and a STOP line (see Chapter 3) and may not be used in any other circumstances. Two sizes are prescribed. (See Table A below).

5.132 The marking should normally be located so that the top edge of the word is not more than 2,750mm nor less than 2,100mm from the nearest part of the double STOP line. Exceptionally this distance may be increased by up to 15 metres.

### Slow Fig. 5:3(b)

5.133 This marking may be used to supplement any warning sign on the approach to a hazard or a road junction, including the advance signs giving warning of STOP and GIVE WAY (Chapter 3). It should not be used to supplement the GIVE WAY sign alone for which the hollow triangular marking has been prescribed. Three sizes are prescribed. (See Table B below). The largest size may be used to straddle two traffic lanes.

5.134 Discretion should be exercised in the use of the marking to ensure that its impact is not lost by proliferation. At particularly hazardous situations eg on the approach to a bend at the end of a long straight section of high speed road, the marking may be repeated to give added emphasis.

5.135 The location of the marking will depend on the nature of the hazard. In general it should be located sufficiently far back to enable a driver travelling at the normal speed of the road to reduce speed in time to negotiate the hazard in safety. This means that the marking will be usually located alongside its associated warning sign.

Para. 5.136 not allocated

### Bus Stop and Bus Stop Marking
Figs. 5:19(a) and (b)

5.137 These markings delineate the limits of a bus stop and should only be used to supplement a kerbside bus stop sign. They carry no mandatory significance to drivers of other vehicles; yellow waiting restriction markings along the edge of the carriageway are necessary if waiting is to be restricted.

5.138 Where the stop serves frequent or multiple services or vehicles with different entrance positions the length of the bay in Fig. 5:19(a) may be increased as necessary in stages of 2 metres from a minimum of 19 metres to a maximum of 39 metres. The legend Bus Stop should be repeated if the bay is extended 12m or more in excess of the minimum length. The lettering and border markings are normally white but where the marking is provided on a road subject to a

**TABLE A**

| Overall Height | Overall Width | Use |
|---|---|---|
| 1,600mm | 2,050mm | Associated with 750mm STOP sign |
| 2,800mm | 2,050mm | Associated with 900mm and 1,200mm STOP signs |

**TABLE B**

| Overall Height | Overall Width | Use |
|---|---|---|
| 1,600mm | 2,280mm | Normal single lane approach |
| 2,800mm | 2,280mm | High speed single lane approach |
| 4,200mm | 3,420mm | High speed approach, half width of road 5 metres or more |

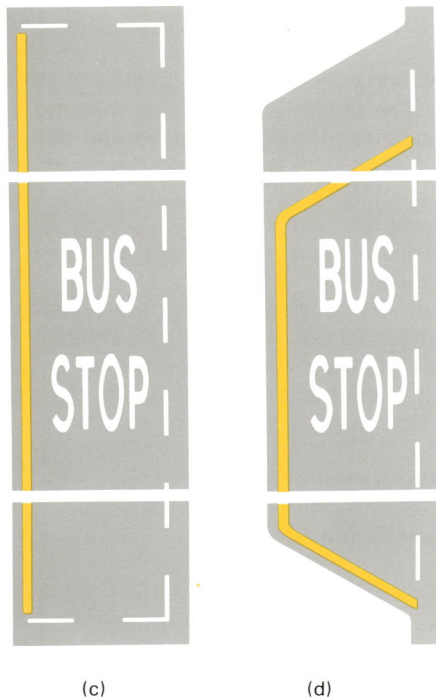

(c)          (d)

**Fig. 5:19**
Bus Stop Clearway markings

single or double yellow waiting restriction line the marking must also be yellow.

**Bus Stop Clearways** Figs. 5:19(c) and (d)

5.139 Their application and use are dealt with under Clearways in Chapter 3—Regulatory signs. Details of materials and the application of these markings are given in Sections 16 and 17 of this Chapter.

**Keep Clear** Fig. 5:20

5.140 This marking indicates to drivers that part of the carriageway at the road junctions which should be left clear of stationary vehicles so as to permit the passage of vehicles into or out of a side turning. Its main use is in urban areas where a queue of vehicles waiting at one junction may block back across a previous junction and thereby obstruct the flow of cross traffic.

5.141 The marking is not intended to keep areas of the carriageway outside premises clear of waiting vehicles.

5.142 not allocated.

**Fig. 5:20** (Diag. 1026)

### Box Junction Road Markings

5.143 A Traffic Regulation Order must be made by the Local Highway Authority before a Box Junction road marking can be put down.

5.144 GENERAL. At a box junction, the carriageway is marked with yellow lines to form a box enclosing yellow cross hatched diagonal lines. Drivers whose vehicles enter the boxed areas when other stationary vehicles are preventing them from leaving it are committing an offence unless queueing to turn right, and then prevented from leaving the junction only by moving traffic or by other vehicles waiting to complete the right turn. It is also an offence to remain stationary in the box when endeavouring to make a right turn if the exit in that direction is blocked. Experience shows that the markings have increased traffic flows where previously there had been delays due to vehicles blocking back across the junction and impeding the cross flow. At signal controlled junctions the queues of traffic left at the end of a green phase have been significantly reduced and there have been marked reductions in injury accidents at the junctions, especially in accidents involving pedestrians.
Box markings are no substitute for traffic signals and they do not solve right turning problems. They are simply an aid to traffic flow at a junction where blocking back affecting a cross flow is a significant problem. Special uses are dealt with in para. 5.149.

5.145 SUITABLE JUNCTIONS. Not all junctions are suitable for treatment and it is necessary to apply certain criteria before deciding whether a particular site should be marked. It will normally be necessary to carry out a traffic survey to determine the extent of the problem, particularly at peak traffic periods, so as to determine not only the suitability of the junction for box marking but also to determine whether any other remedial measures might be effective (eg linking of traffic signals with those at adjacent junctions).

5.146 FACTORS IN DECISION. Factors which influence a decision to provide box markings include the following:—

(a) The junction should preferably, though not necessarily, be controlled by signals.

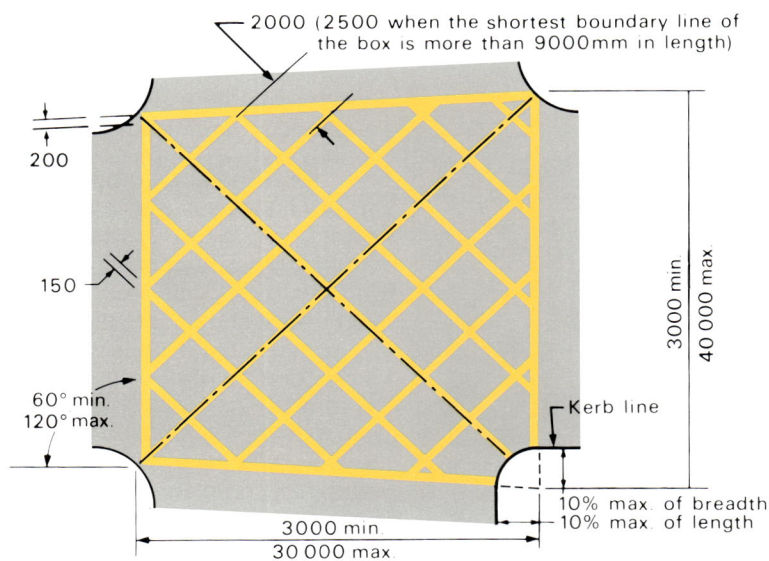

2000 (2500 when the shortest boundary line of the box is more than 9000mm in length)

200

150

60° min.
120° max.

3000 min
40 000 max

Kerb line

3000 min
30 000 max.

10% max. of breadth
10% max. of length

(a)
**Full box**

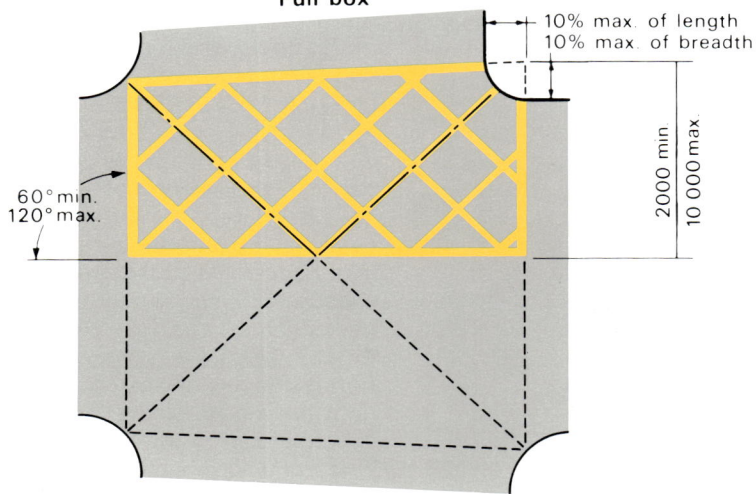

10% max. of length
10% max. of breadth

60° min.
120° max.

2000 min
10 000 max.

(b)
**Half box**

## NOTES

1. This drawing shows typical layouts of the markings. The overall shape of the marking and the number of oblique lines should be varied to accord with the circumstances at the site.

2. To set out the markings on the carriageway:
    (a) Set out the diagonals at right angles (or as near as possible) to each other.
    (b) Complete the boundary lines.
    (c) Set out remaining lines parallel to diagonals, at grid intervals of 2,000mm.

3. Half boxes should be constructed as for a full box but with only half the markings shown. See Figure B.

4. Markings at more complicated junctions where varying widths of road produce boundaries which are not rectangles, should be constructed as follows:
    (a) Draw transverse lines across the entry arm of the junction approximately at right angles to the flow of traffic.
    (b) Complete the perimeter of the box by following the intervening kerb lines.
    (c) Draw a main diagonal x−y.
    (d) By construction draw in the other diagonal p−q. The two diagonals should intersect as nearly as possible at right angles.
    (e) Complete the box in accordance with Note 2.

The method of constructing this type of marking is illustrated in Figures C and D.

5. A full box marking is sometimes required which is much longer than it is wide. In this case it should be constructed as for a half box as illustrated in Figure E.

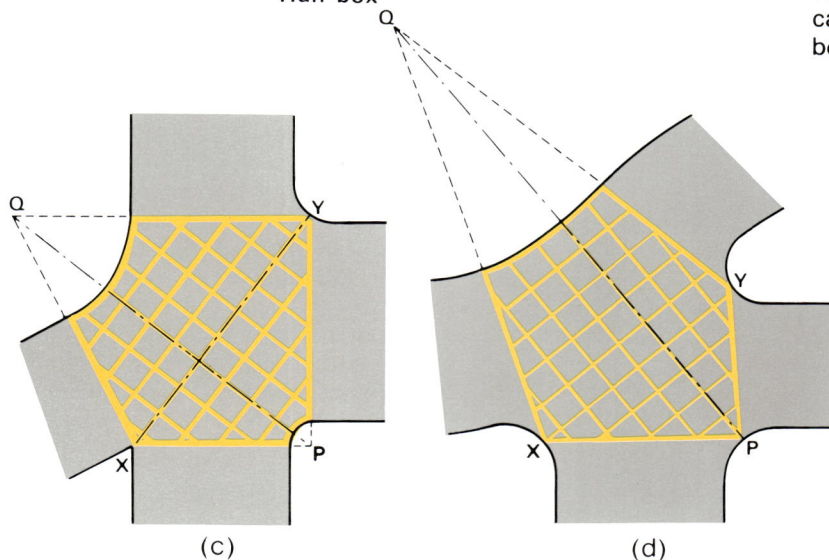

(c)

(d)

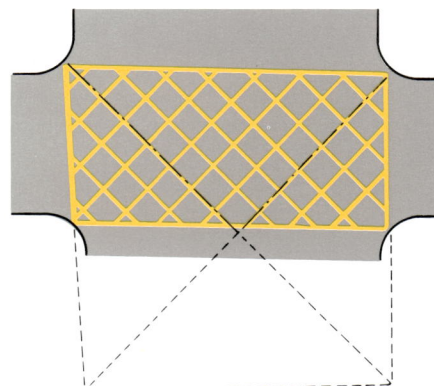

(e)

# Fig. 5:21 (Diag. 1043 & 1044)
Box junction carriageway markings

(b) Blocking back from a junction ahead should occur under existing conditions even for short periods.

(c) Preferably there should be heavy traffic flows on both opposing arms of the junction (at intersections with minor roads where blocking of the mouth of the minor road is infrequent, a 'Keep Clear' road marking may meet the need).

(d) Entrances to and exits from the junction should normally be opposite each other. The markings may, however, be used exceptionally at staggered junctions, particularly where the minor roads have a right-hand stagger, provided the maximum box length of 30 metres is not exceeded and irregular shapes can be avoided. Two half boxes may be a practical substitute for one large box in such circumstances.

(e) Generally there should be at least two lanes on each major road approach.

(f) The carriageway beyond the junction should be free from obstruction (this may necessitate the imposition of waiting restrictions and/or loading restrictions or the adjustment of bus stops on the lengths concerned).

(g) Where a succession of junctions gives rise to blocking back, consideration should be given to the establishment of a series of boxes, having regard to the storage space between the junctions. Where junctions are closely spaced, box markings should be considered even if blocking back occurs only for short periods, provided at least 20 metres storage space can be maintained between each successive box.

(h) Special consideration needs to be given to junctions where there is a high proportion of right turning traffic since experience has shown that the value of the marking is reduced under these conditions.

5.147 HALF BOXES—the use of half boxes (in which only half the area of the junction is marked) is appropriate at 'T' junctions and other junctions where traffic only blocks back from one direction. Half boxes may be used only in the position illustrated in Fig. 5:22.

5.148 ROAD MARKINGS—details of the road markings are given in Fig. 5:21. Two diagonal lines join opposite corners, or projected corners, of the box and lines are drawn parallel to each diagonal to form cross hatched marking in yellow. The diagonal lines 150mm wide are spaced 2,000mm apart where the shortest boundary line of the box is 9,000mm or less, and 2,500mm apart where the shortest boundary line of the box is more than 9,000mm. Box junctions must always have four straight sides transverse to the traffic flow on the approaches, although up to 10% of the length of any side may be cut away as shown in the diagrams to accommodate corner kerbs. The overall shape of the marking and the number of cross hatching/lines will vary to accord with the circumstances at the site. Where the intersecting carriageways are of a different width the shortest boundary line of the box is taken as the determining factor for the spacing (x) between the parallel cross hatching lines. Where the shortest boundary line of the box is 9,000mm or less in length, $x = 2,000$mm. Where the shortest boundary of the box is more than 9,000mm in length, $x = 2,500$mm. Width of markings:— Boundary Lines—200mm, Cross Hatching—150mm. To set out the markings on the carriageway:—

1. Complete the boundary lines.
2. Set out the diagonals.
3. Set out remaining lines parallel to diagonals.

**Fig. 5:22**
Half-box at 'T' junction

| overall width of carriageway (metres) | traffic flow |
|---|---|
| 5.0—5.9 | 500 |
| 6.0—7.4 | 600 |
| 7.5 | 750 |

Any proposals for non-quadrilateral shapes must be referred to Regional Controllers (R&T) before any action is taken.

Half box markings should be designed in the same way as full box markings but only half of the box marked on the road—Fig. 5:21(b).

### 5.149 Special Cases

(i) Yellow Box markings should be provided at A.H.B. level crossings if the traffic flow in any one direction exceeds that shown in adjoining table.

(ii) Box junctions may occasionally be useful in narrow streets slightly offset from the actual junction to provide gaps in queueing traffic for long turning vehicles from side roads to negotiate sharp corners. Such use will require special authorisation from the Director (Transport).

(iii) Box junction markings have occasionally proved useful in combination with priority signs (see Chapter 3) to break queues through an exceptionally narrow pinch point, to enable an opposing flow to continue without unnecessary delay. Special authorisation is required.

NB: Box junctions may not be laid at roundabouts nor to cater for merging movements.

### School Keep Clear Fig. 5:23(a & b)

5.150 The marking consists of the words SCHOOL KEEP CLEAR painted on the carriageway in 700mm yellow letters with a zig-zag pattern of yellow lines the overall length of which should not be less than 25.56m. The overall length of the marking may be increased by increments of 6m by the addition of a complete zig-zag pattern on each side of the marking up to a maximum of 43.56m. The marking is intended as a reminder not to park at the school entrance, whether the driver has business at the school or is merely seeking parking space.

5.151 The length of the marking needs to be restricted to one which drivers will respect. Where an authority desires to lay a marking with an overall length greater than the maximum of 43.56 metres, eg where the school is in a cul-de-sac or where the marking is to extend across two entrances which are wide apart, then two markings of any of the standard lengths, ie 25.56m, 31.56m, 37.56 or 43.56m, may be joined together omitting the transverse bars at the join to form one continuous marking.

5.152 Where two separate markings (either single or double as described above) are required to be laid in close proximity for school entrances on the same side of a length of road, a clear space of 7 metres must be left between the markings.

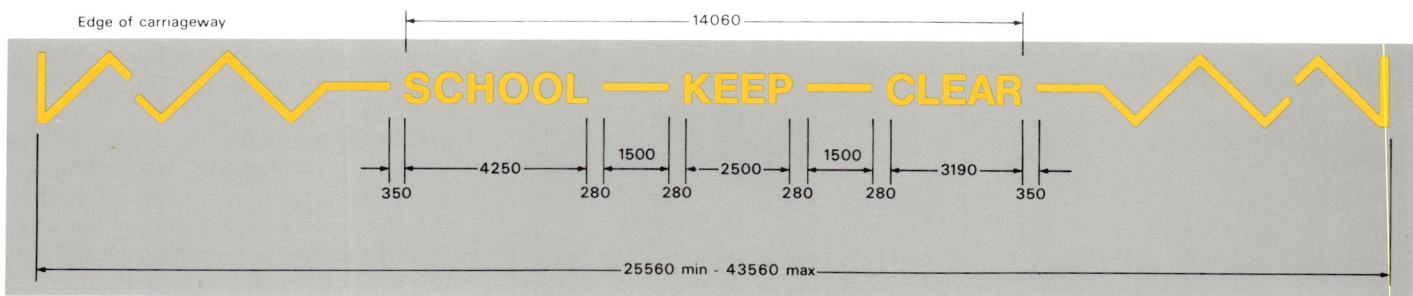

**Fig. 5:23** (Diag. 1027.1) (a)

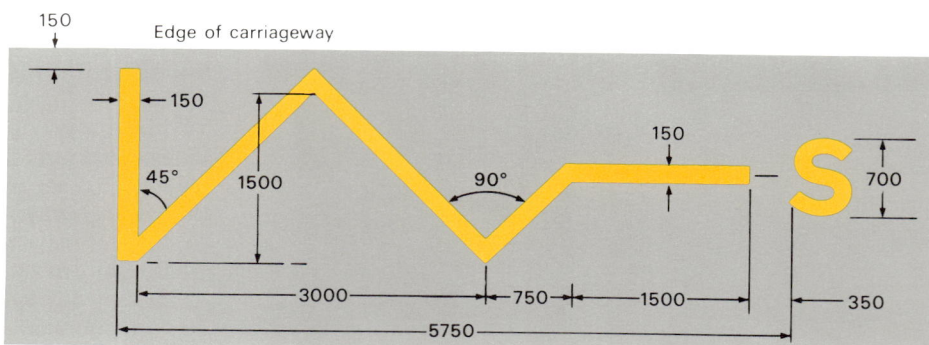

(b)

44

5.153 The marking should not normally be placed on both sides of the road but only the side on which the entrance is situated. However, when school entrances occur opposite, or nearly opposite each other, and there is a case for providing the markings at each entrance, then, they may be laid on both sides subject to the approval of the Director (Transport).

5.154 The markings should not be laid in the controlled areas on the approaches to Zebra crossings, but where waiting restrictions are in force there is no objection to both the School Keep Clear marking and the yellow lines denoting the waiting restrictions being used along the same length of road.

5.155 It is not intended that the markings should be used outside all schools, but only where there is a clear need for them because of the hazard to school children due to parked vehicles. Highway Authorities should therefore ensure that the markings are restricted to sites where they are really necessary in the interests of road safety.

5.156 Guardrails are considered to be the best means of protecting children

at the entrance to schools and should be provided wherever appropriate even though the carriageway markings are also used.

5.157 Fire and Ambulance stations Fig. 5:24. Where problems of obstructions arise at the entrances to Hospitals, Ambulance Stations or Fire Stations the School Keep Clear marking Fig. 5:23a may be adapted by the omission of the legend SCHOOL. In these cases the overall minimum size of the marking is reduced to 25.25 and the maximum size 43.25. The advice given in paras 5.151, 5.152 and 5.153 is equally applicable.

**Taxis** Fig. 5:25

5.158 Two forms of marking are prescribed for approved taxi ranks according to whether they are at the side or in the centre of the carriageway. The length of the 'box' comprising the marking may be varied to suit the requirements.
The lettering and border markings are normally white but where the marking is provided on a road subject to a single or double yellow waiting restriction line the marking must also be yellow.

**Fig. 5:24** (Diag 1027.1)
KEEP CLEAR markings for situations other than at Schools

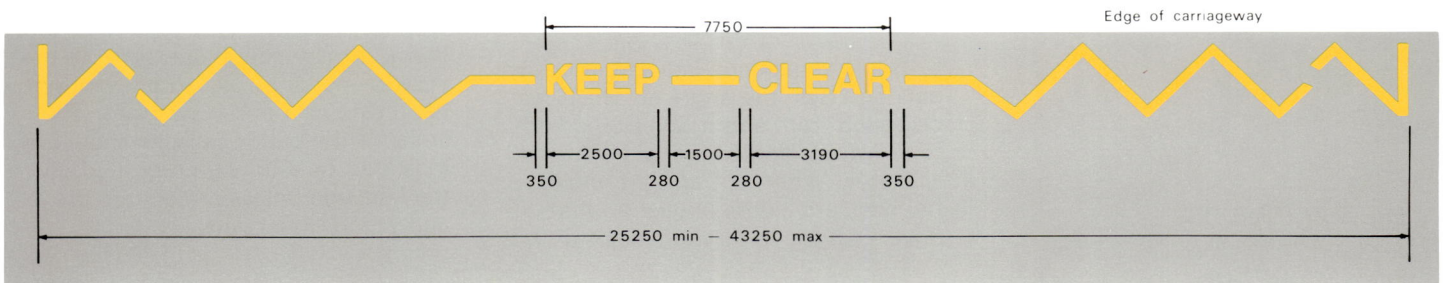

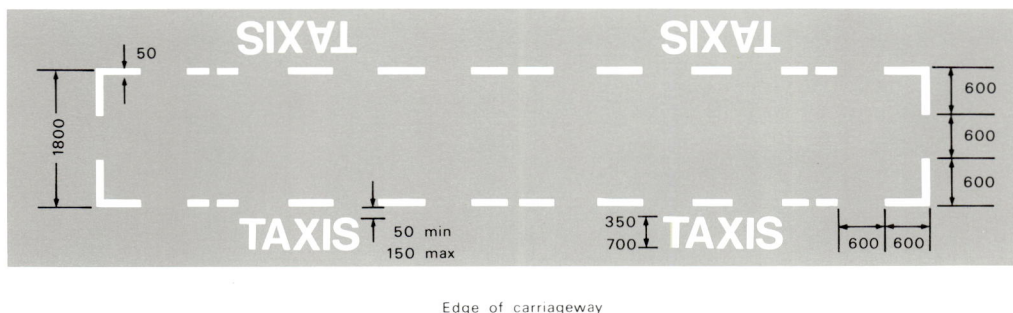

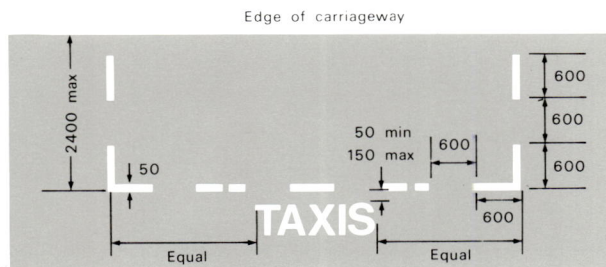

**Fig. 5:25** (Diag. 1028.1)

**Parking Bays** Figs. 5:26 and 5:27

5.159 Two patterns of marking are prescribed, one to indicate the limits for parallel parking and one for angled parking bays. Both types of marking may be used outside or inside controlled parking zones.

5.160 The markings may only be used to indicate the limits of designated on-street parking places established under Sections 28 or 35 of the Road Traffic Regulation Act 1967. They must always be accompanied by upright signs carrying a 'P' symbol together with the conditions that

apply at the parking places unless parking meters are present. (Details of these signs are given in Chapter 2— Informatory Signs).

**Parallel Parking** Fig. 5:26

5.161 The double broken terminal markings indicate the limits of the space reserved for vehicle parking which should also be denoted by 'P' signs mounted at the kerbside. The single broken transverse lines between individual parking spaces may be used if desired or may be omitted.

**Fig. 5:26** (Diag. 1032)
Limits of Parallel Parking

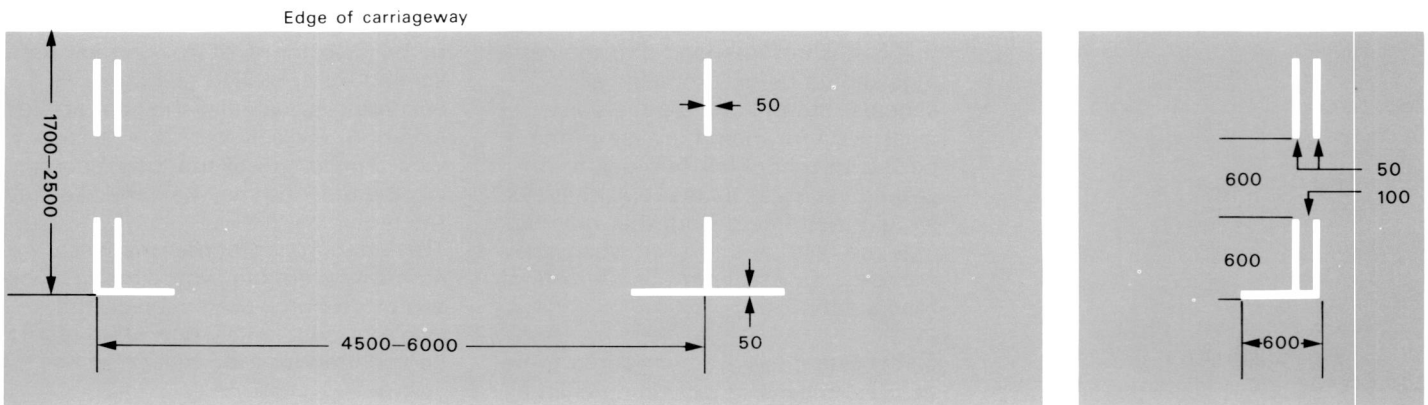

**Angled Parking** Fig. 5:27

5.162 The markings indicate individual parking bays, the angle of which may be varied from about 30° to the kerb to 90° according to the width of road available. When not at right angles the bays should be angled so that drivers on the left hand side of a two-

way carriageway need to reverse into them. Similar conditions apply in the case of markings placed on the right hand side of a one-way street. The limits of the parking places should be indicated by a 'P' sign mounted on the kerbside unless meters are provided at individual bays.

**Fig. 5:27** (Diag. 1033)
Angled Parking Bays

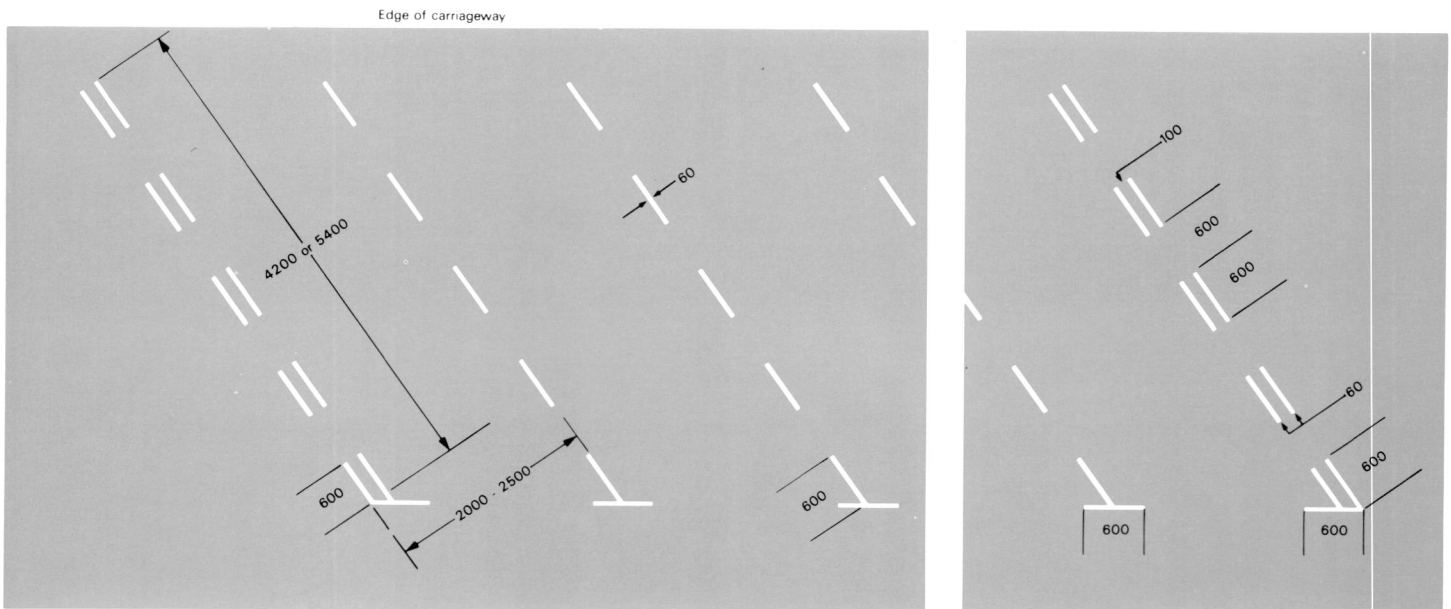

**Look Left/Right** Fig. 5:28

5.163 This marking is intended to warn pedestrians of approaching vehicular traffic in a one-way street. The marking consists of the words LOOK LEFT or LOOK RIGHT painted on the carriageway in 280mm white letters and is usually provided at sites where pedestrians are encouraged to cross by the provision of pedestrian refuges and where traffic is approaching from the opposite direction than the one they might expect.

**Bus Lanes**

5.164 The markings prescribed for use in lanes reserved for buses without physical separation are shown in Figs. 5:29 and 5:30.
They are used in conjunction with other road markings described elsewhere in this chapter (ie Figs. 5:7, 5:13a and 5:37) and various upright signs which are described in detail in Chapter 3.

5.165 Bus lanes may be either (i) with-flow, or (ii) contra-flow, and typical arrangements of the markings used in each case are illustrated in Figs. 5:31 and 5:32.

5.166 **With-Flow Bus Lanes**
(i) The outer edge of the bus lane should be marked by a white line to Fig. 5:30(a), a gap being left in the line adjacent to each side road.

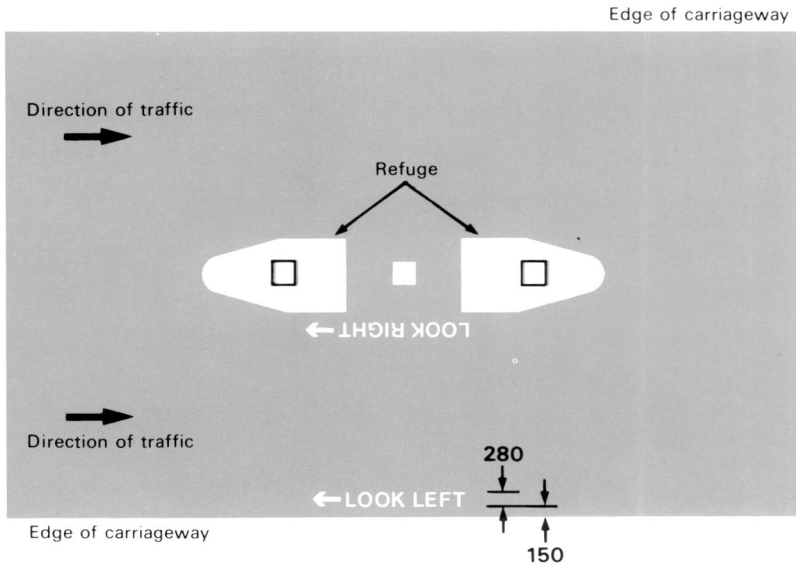

**Fig. 5:28** (Diag. 1029)
Look Left/Right markings

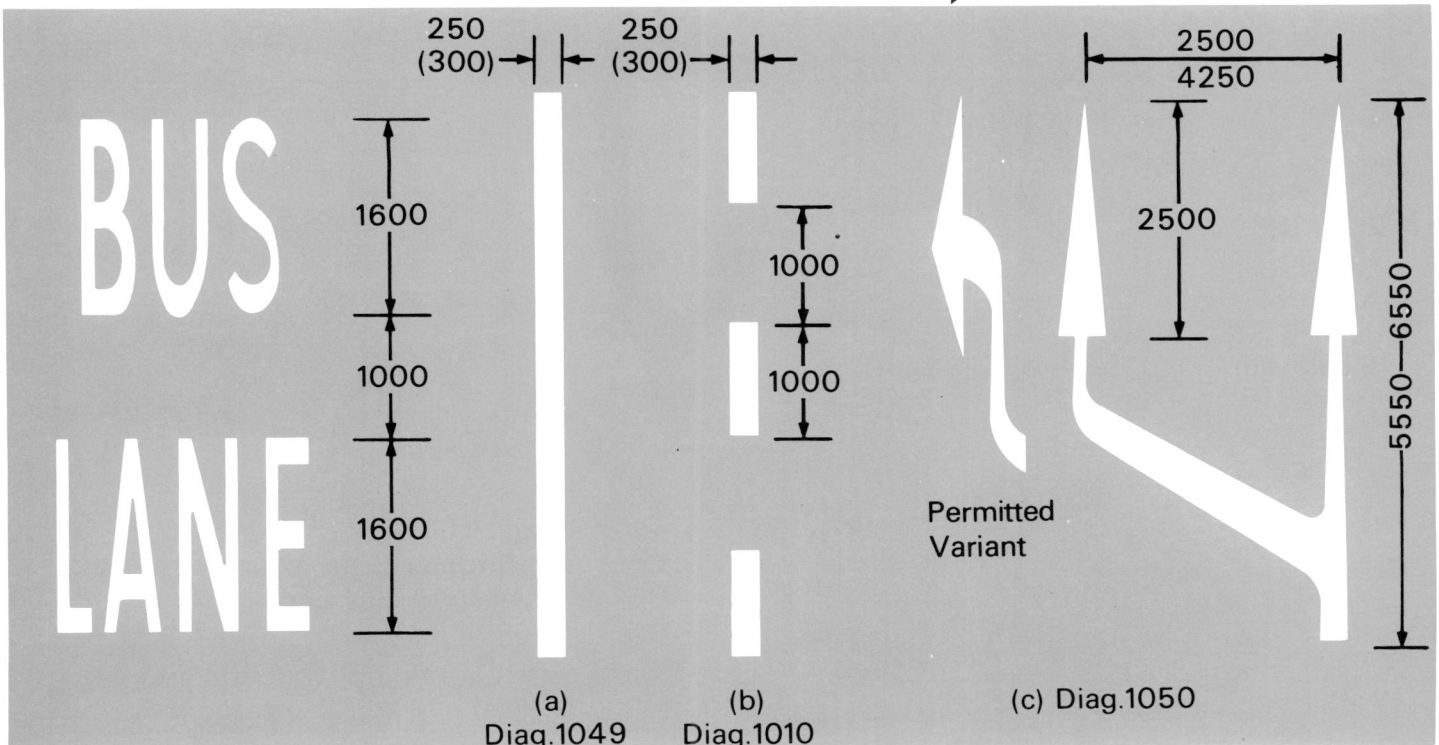

**Fig. 5:29** (Diag. 1048)

**Fig. 5:30**
Other markings used with BUS LANES

## Fig. 5.31
Road Markings for Kerbside With-Flow bus lane

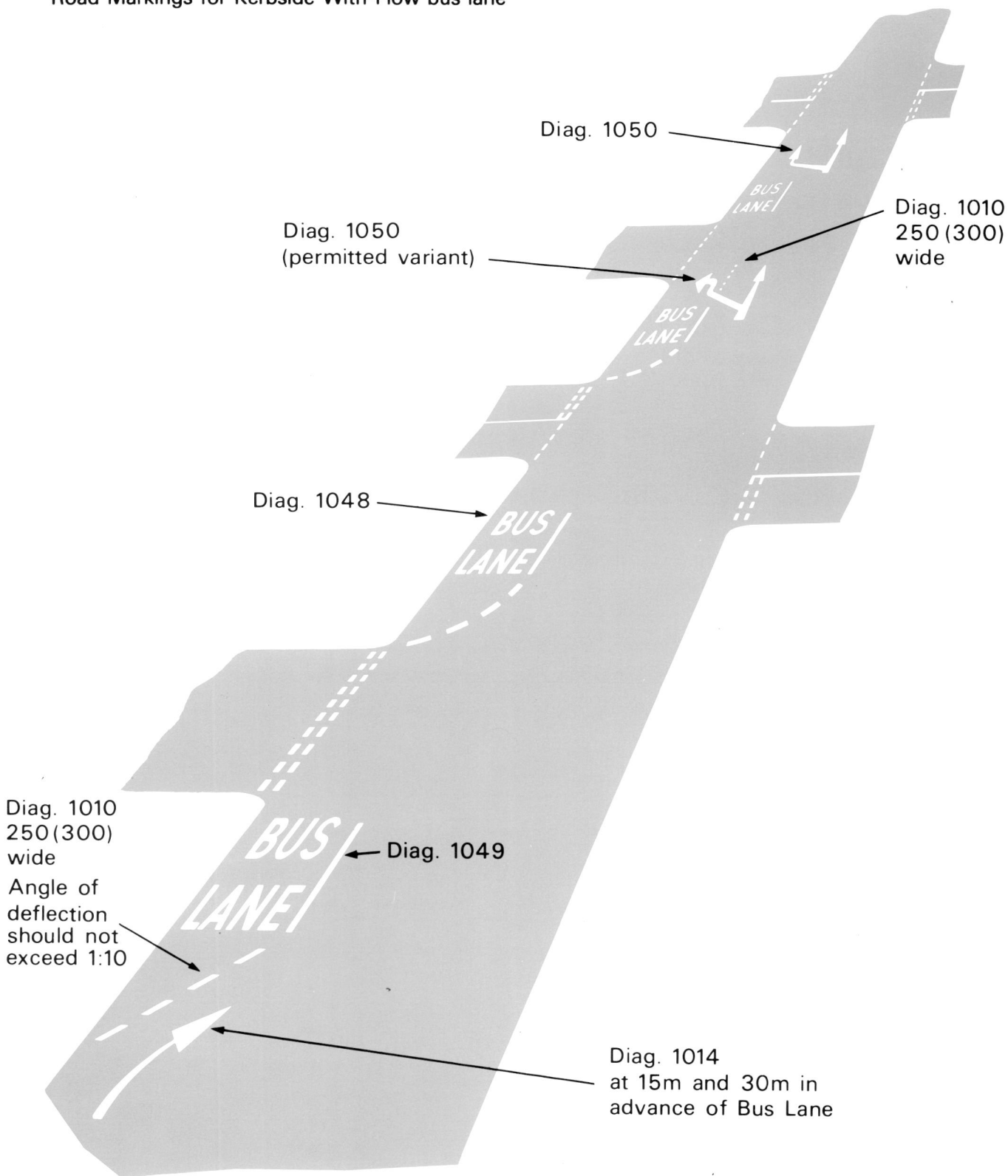

Diag. 1050

Diag. 1010
250 (300)
wide

Diag. 1050
(permitted variant)

Diag. 1048

Diag. 1010
250 (300)
wide

Angle of
deflection
should not
exceed 1:10

Diag. 1049

Diag. 1014
at 15m and 30m in
advance of Bus Lane

The legend BUS LANE Fig. 5:29 should be marked on the carriageway across the lane at its commencement and repeated after each junction. Where junctions are more than 300 metres apart the road markings should be repeated between junctions at approximately 150 metres intervals. Warning arrows Fig. 5:7, should be placed on the nearside lane 15 metres and 30 metres in advance of the commencement of the bus lane. A 250mm wide broken line to diagram 5:13a should be laid from the kerb to the start of the full width lane to deflect other traffic from the bus lane. The taper at which the line should be laid should not normally exceed 1:10.

5.167 In some circumstances a 1:10 taper would not be appropriate. For example, along a left-hand bend such a taper would not appear as pronounced as it would along a straight length of carriageway and on lengths of road where frequent side road junctions occur a taper shorter than the normal 1:10 is essential in order to avoid encroaching upon the mouth of a side road. For such sites therefore, the angle of taper may be reduced, but in no circumstances should it be less than 1:5. On right-hand bends where a foreshortening effect is apparent, no reduction in the length of the normal taper, of 1:10 is recommended.

5.168 Where a bus lane commences just beyond a junction, adequate length should be left for the taper to commence at the junction so that the inclined line does not extend across the junction mouth. Similarly to allow traffic to position itself correctly on the carriageway, the continuous line should end in advance of any junction with a major left-turning flow. In this case the continuous line should be replaced by a broken line to Fig. 5:30(b) and should be preceded by the double headed arrow variant, Fig. 5:30(c) to inform motorists that it is permissible to enter the bus lane prior to making the left-turn.

5.169 Beyond each junction carrying emerging traffic, a curved line to Fig. 5:30(b) should be provided across the bus lane to continue the line of a normal left-turn out of the side road and at the end of a bus lane the normal double headed arrow Fig. 5:30(c) may be used.

5.170 **Contra-Flow Bus Lanes**
(ii) The road markings are as in Figs. 5:29 and 5:30 with a continuous line to Fig. 5:30(a) separating the BUS LANE from other lanes. In normal cases the 250mm wide line is used, but where road safety considerations require that special emphasis be given the 300mm wide line may be used.

5.171 Road markings to Fig. 5:29 together with an appropriate direction arrow to Fig. 5:37 should be sited so as to be legible to drivers emerging from side roads. Similarly road markings to Fig. 5:28 should be used at known pedestrian crossing points, to warn pedestrians that traffic is not approaching from the normal direction.

5.172 Generally a basic width of 3 metres is required for a bus lane. The distance is measured from the edge of the kerb to the centre of the continuous white line. A narrower bus lane may be a danger to pedestrians on the footway and may also force buses to travel slower than is necessary. At pinch-points narrower bus lanes may need to be accepted but the lane width should never be less than 2.8 metres.

**Fig. 5:32**
Road Markings for Contra-Flow bus lane

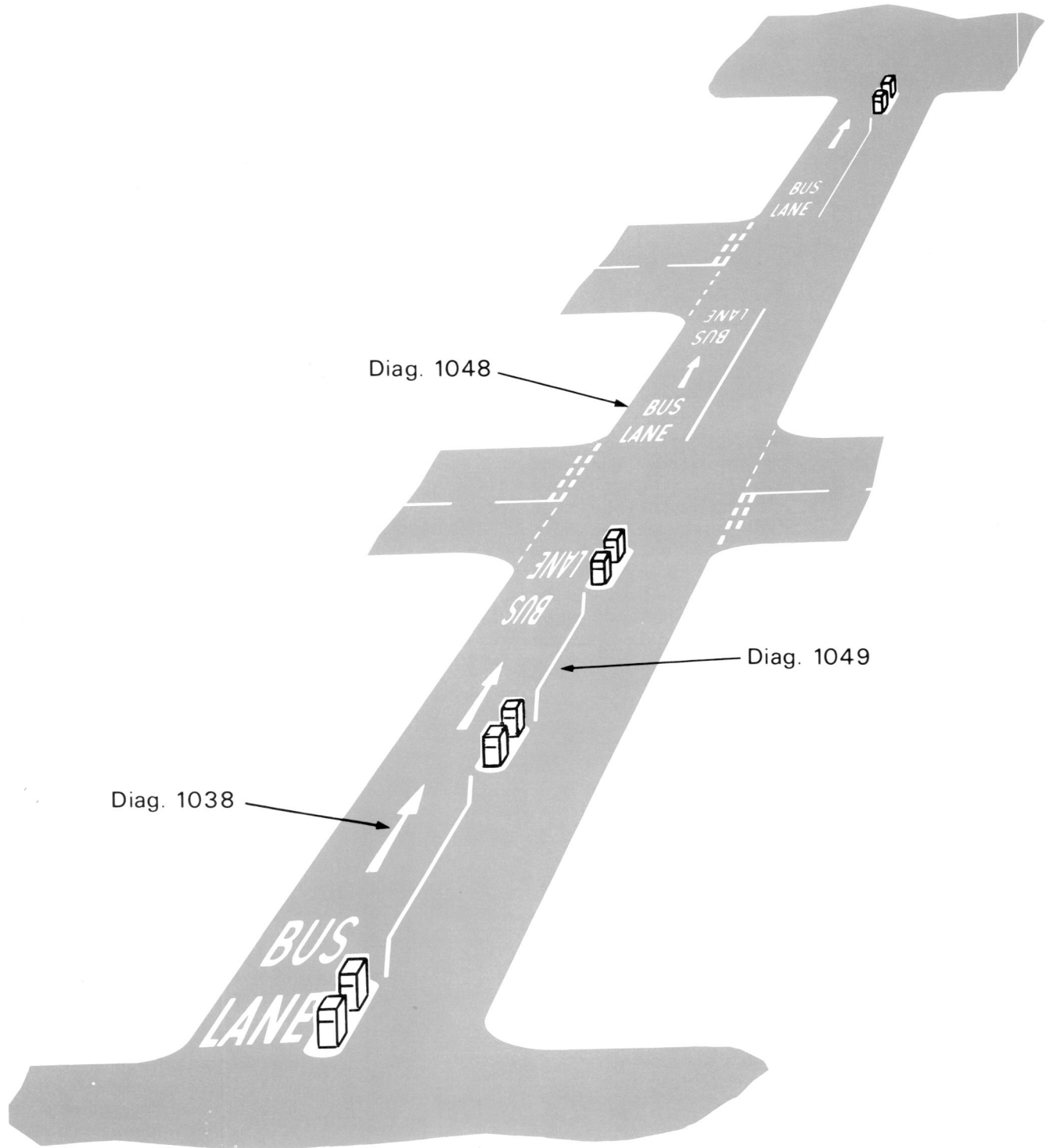

Diag. 1048

Diag. 1049

Diag. 1038

**Fig. 5:33**
Markings for Cycle Lanes

**(a)**

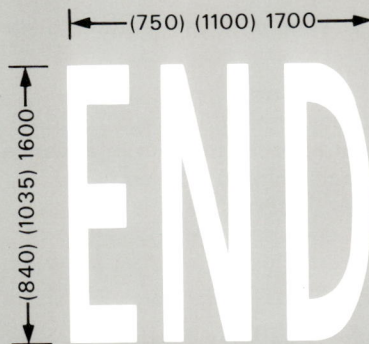

**(b)**

**(c)**

### Road Markings for Cyclists
Fig. 5:33

5.173 The recommended markings are prescribed in the Traffic Signs (Amendment) Regulations 1982.

5.174 The markings are white in colour and are used to advise cyclists of the route to take in cases where local authorities have introduced special facilities for cyclists.

5.175 The cycle symbol Fig. 5:33a is available in three sizes and can be used in: —

(i) Cycle tracks, ie special tracks for cyclists parallel to but physically separated from roads used by motor traffic. It should be supplemented in these cases by upright signs to Diag. 625.

(ii) Cycleways, ie tracks for cyclists entirely distinct from the road system. Again it should be supplemented by upright signs to Diag. 625.

(iii) Cycle lanes, ie lanes allocated for the exclusive use of cyclists. These are delineated by a 150mm wide continuous white line. For a with-flow lane upright signs based on those used for *bus lanes* would be appropriate to supplement the carriageway markings. If a contra-flow cycle lane is proposed special signing treatment will be required to ensure that danger to cyclists is kept to a minimum.

(iv) Segregated Cycle track foot-path, ie a special track divided by a physical barrier or by a 150mm wide continuous white line to provide separate paths for pedestrians and cycles. The cycle symbol should be applied to the cycle path and supplemented by upright signs to Fig. 5:34(b) which also require to be specially authorised.

(v) Advisory cycle routes, ie all purpose generally minor roads which cyclists are encouraged to use by the display of signs to Diag. 815 or specially authorised cycle direction signs. The cycle symbol may be laid at intervals along such roads and at simple junctions and it may be supplemented by a small direction arrow marking (reduced version of Fig. 5:37) to indicate the route cyclists should take.

5.176 The termination of a prescribed cycle lane or track should be indicated by an END marking on the carriageway Fig. 5:33b. This must always be used in conjunction with the cycle symbol as illustrated in Fig. 5:33c.

5.177 Cycle ways or tracks crossing minor roads may be indicated on the carriageway by a special road marking Fig. 5:34(a). This marking is purely informatory and does not confer any priority on cyclists.

5.178 Half size GIVE WAY markings and 2000mm long direction arrows pointing ahead or to the left or right as required, may be authorised for use where appropriate, on cycle tracks and cycleways.

5.179 and 5.180 not allocated.

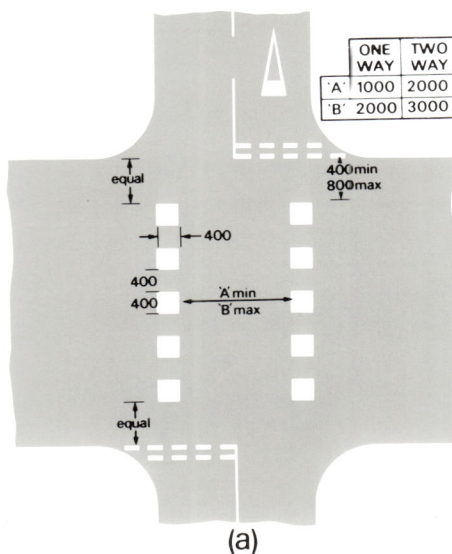

| | ONE WAY | TWO WAY |
|---|---|---|
| 'A' | 1000 | 2000 |
| 'B' | 2000 | 3000 |

(a)

(b)

**Fig. 5:34**

# 13. Marking of Signal Controlled and Other Junctions

## Signal Controlled Junction
## Figs. 5:35 and 5:36

5.181 Adequate and proper marking of the approaches to signal controlled junctions is essential if the signals are to operate at their maximum efficiency.
The requirements are:—

(a) The STOP line must be sited as near as practical to the intersection, consistent with vehicle and pedestrian needs, and drivers waiting at the STOP line must have an uninterrupted view of at least one signal;

(b) Lane lines must be arranged to secure the maximum use of available carriageway space consistent with adequate lane width;

(c) Drivers need to be given guidance as to the correct lane to take in good time before reaching the junction.

5.182 Fig. 5:35 shows in detail the standard layout of the STOP lines, primary signals and controlled pedestrian crossings at a signal controlled junction having differing numbers of lanes on each approach.

5.183 Fig. 5:36 shows a typical arrangement of lane and centre of carriageway markings for a six lane road subject to a 40 mph (60 kph) speed limit at a signal controlled junction with a four lane road subject to a 30 mph (50 kph) speed limit.

5.184 Dealing with the features mentioned:—

(i) **Stop lines.** These are dealt with in Section 4. The STOP line is normally located 1m in advance of the left hand side primary signal. It should normally be at right angles to the centre line of the carriageway, even at skew junctions.

(ii) **Lane lines.** Two patterns of marking are used, the normal lane and centre of carriageway markings on the distant approach which change to warning line markings on the near approach to the signals.

5.185 The pattern of the warning marking is either the Urban or Rural type of warning lines (see para 5.64). The choice of marking at particular sites depends on the speed value of the road.

5.186 The centre warning line on four or six lane carriageways is 150mm in width. Elsewhere the warning lines are 100mm wide.

5.187 The number of marks comprising the warning lines depends on the degree of congestion at the site and on the speeds and volume of traffic. The recommended minimum number of marks is given in Table B.

(iii) **Lane widths.**

5.188 The normal width of the lanes should be 3m—3.6m depending on the

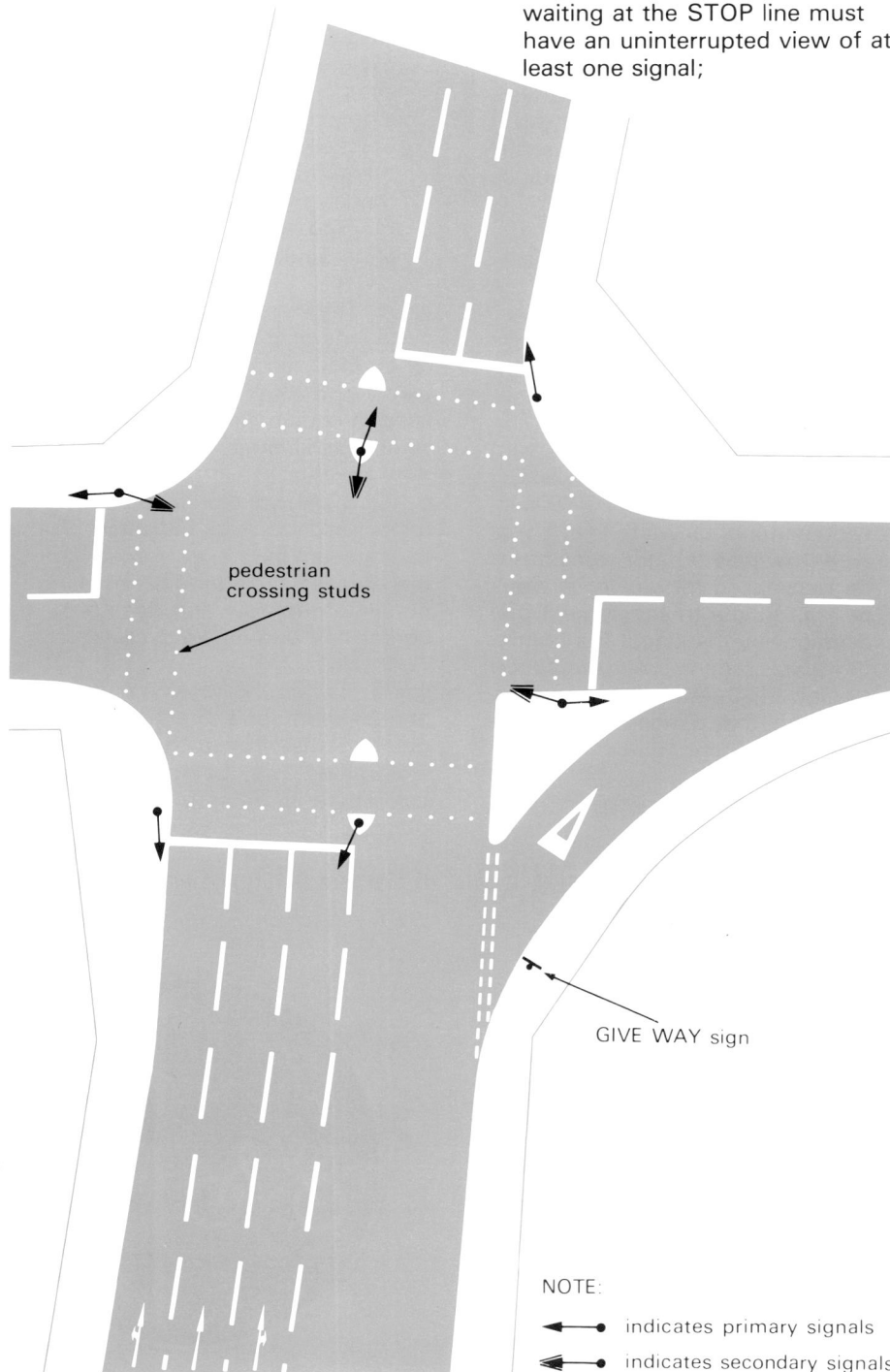

pedestrian crossing studs

GIVE WAY sign

NOTE:

◀━━━ indicates primary signals

◀━━━ indicates secondary signals

**Fig. 5:35**
Layout of signal controlled junction

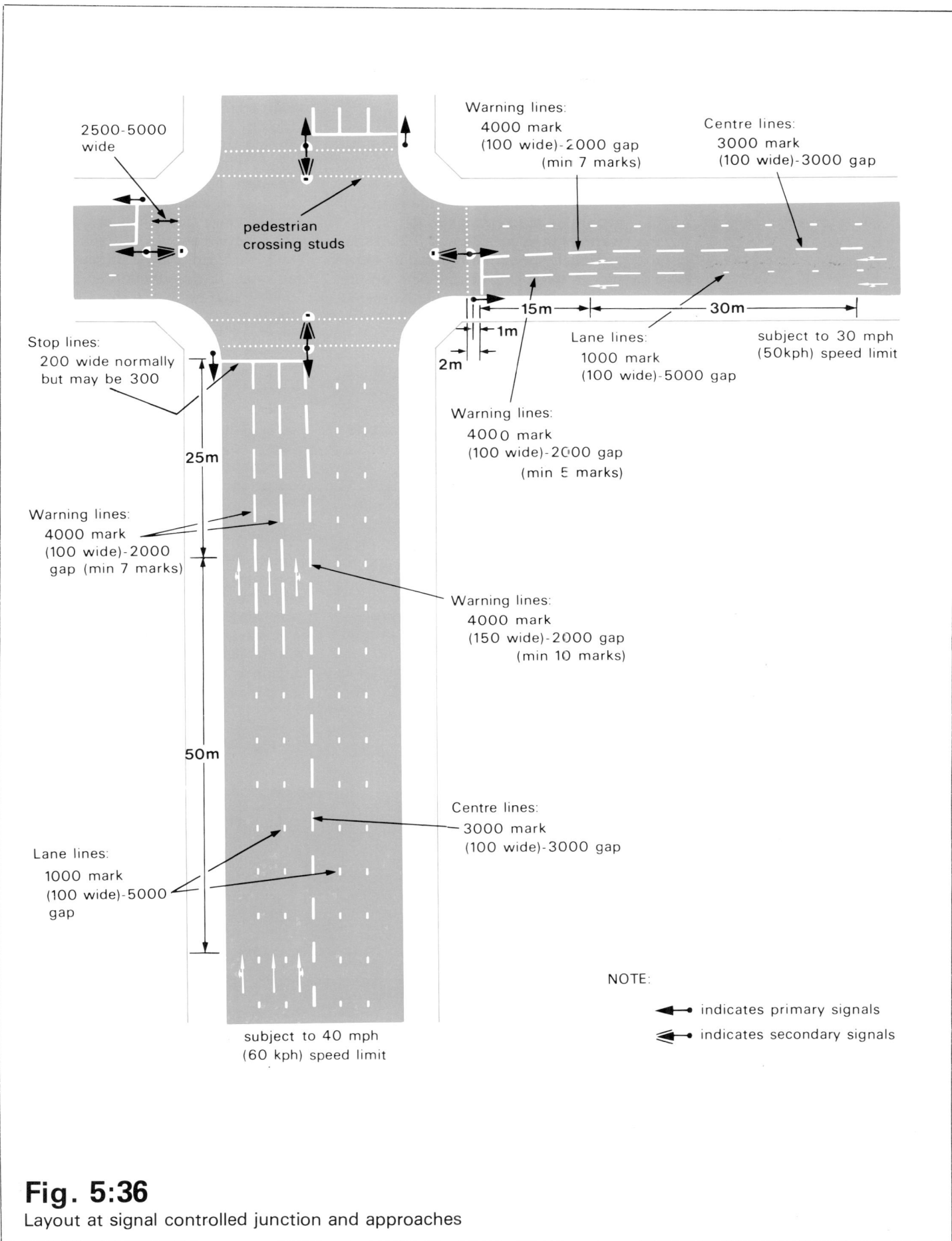

**2500-5000 wide**

**pedestrian crossing studs**

**Warning lines:**
4000 mark
(100 wide)-2000 gap
(min 7 marks)

**Centre lines:**
3000 mark
(100 wide)-3000 gap

**Stop lines:**
200 wide normally
but may be 300

15m

30m

1m

2m

**Lane lines:**
1000 mark
(100 wide)-5000 gap

subject to 30 mph
(50kph) speed limit

**Warning lines:**
4000 mark
(100 wide)-2000 gap
(min 5 marks)

25m

**Warning lines:**
4000 mark
(100 wide)-2000
gap (min 7 marks)

**Warning lines:**
4000 mark
(150 wide)-2000 gap
(min 10 marks)

50m

**Centre lines:**
3000 mark
(100 wide)-3000 gap

**Lane lines:**
1000 mark
(100 wide)-5000
gap

NOTE:

◄━● indicates primary signals

◄◄━● indicates secondary signals

subject to 40 mph
(60 kph) speed limit

# Fig. 5:36
Layout at signal controlled junction and approaches

type and speed of traffic and on the width of carriageway. Exceptionally an absolute minimum width of 2.5m may be accepted alongside refuges at signals and at the STOP line, but not elsewhere.

5.189 Where the approach width is less than 5.2m no lane markings should be provided; for widths between 5.2 and 7.75m the approach should be marked as two lanes; for widths between 7.75 and 8.25m the approach should be marked as either two or three lanes depending on the traffic movements; for widths over 8.25m the approach should be marked as 3 lanes.

5.190 The aim should be to provide the maximum number of lanes on the approach to the intersection but the number of lanes on the leaving side may be reduced due to the dedication of lanes to exclusive turning movements on the approach side. The decision on the number of lanes to adopt will be influenced by safety requirements and will depend on road alignment, traffic movements and the presence of standing vehicles.

(iv) **Lane indication arrows**
Figs. 5:35 and 5:36.

5.191 In addition to the warning lines on the approaches to junctions, direc-tion arrows should be used to give drivers advance indication of the correct lane to take when approaching busy multi-lane intersections, whether signal controlled or not. Generally with speeds less than 40 mph (60 kph) the 4m length of arrow Fig. 5:58(a) should suffice but on open and faster roads the 6m size Fig. 5:58(b) should be used. Normally two arrows should be used in sequence in each lane, occasionally three. The one nearest the junction should be between 15m and 25m from the STOP line, or entrance to the junction and the second should be 30m to 50m further back, the greater distance being used on roads subject to higher average speeds. A third arrow, if used, should be 30m to 50m back from the second arrow. On high speed roads these distances should be increased by up to 50%. The direction of each arrow head may be varied to suit the circumstances but not more than two directions may be shown on any one arrow.

5.192 On two lane approaches to a junction the arrangement of arrows indicating the lanes for (a) straight ahead (b) left-turn and (c) right turn will depend on the relative traffic volumes making the movements and on the site conditions. Where for instance there is a very heavy right turn movement the straight ahead and

**Fig. 5:37** (Diag. 1035)
Destination markings

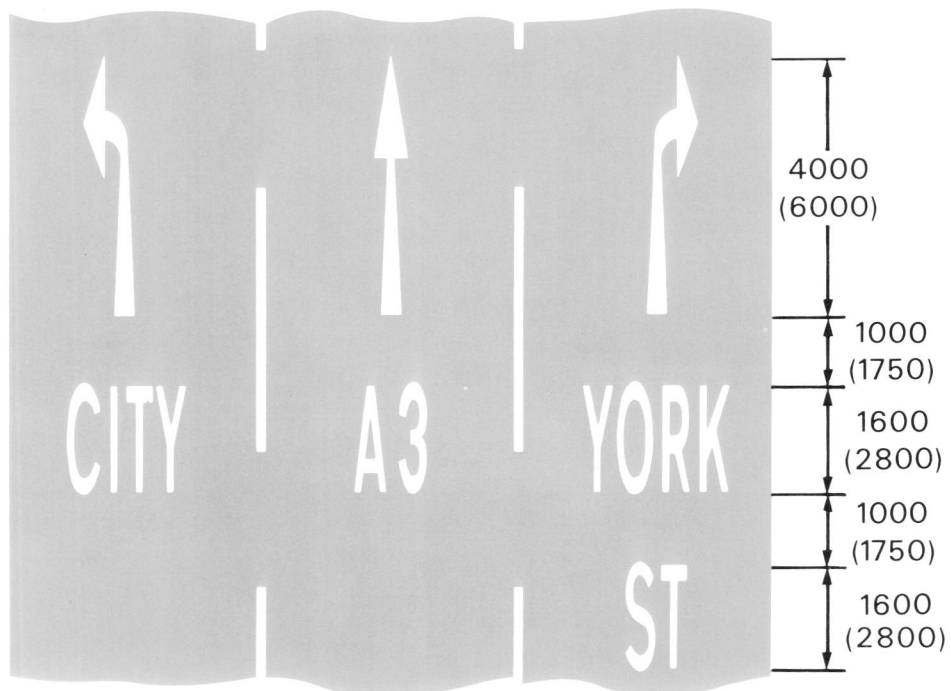

4000
(6000)

1000
(1750)

1600
(2800)

1000
(1750)

1600
(2800)

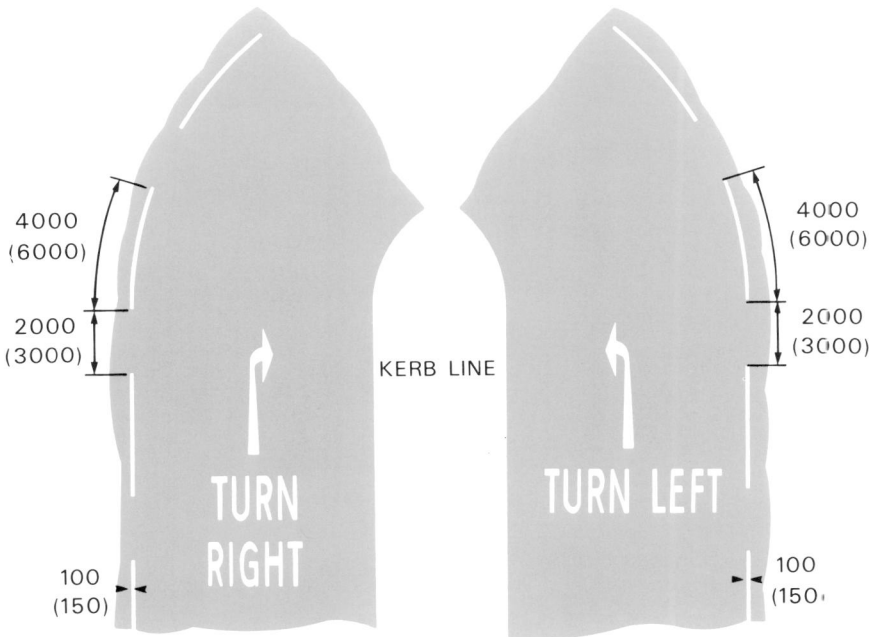

**Fig. 5:38** (Diag. 1036.1)
TURN RIGHT/LEFT markings

5.195 The worded markings TURN RIGHT and TURN LEFT with arrows, Fig. 5:38, may only be used to indicate a compulsory turn. The markings reinforce a green arrow traffic signal indication or a regulatory turn sign. Depending on the carriageway width the marking may be in one or two lanes.

**Other Junctions**

5.196 Markings for typical junction layouts are shown in figures 5:39 to 5:54. Further information on the arrangement of markings at major/minor junctions may be obtained from Departmental Advice Note TA/20/80.

5.197 It will be noted that the hatched markings are all bounded by warning lines and NOT by continuous prohibitory lines. This allows drivers to cross the markings where they can see it is safe to do so.

**Bifurcation Arrows at Deceleration Lanes** Fig. 5:57

5.198 These markings should be provided at the commencement of deceleration lanes on the approaches to junctions.

5.199 Bifurcation Arrows serve to guide vehicles into the deceleration lane near its commencement ensuring that the full length of the lane is used to slow down for the junction without impeding through vehicles on the main carriageway.

5.200 Three sizes are prescribed. The longest (32m) is for use on motorways, the medium (16m) for use on high speed dual carriageway roads and the shortest (8m) for other roads.

5.201 The arrow marking may be transposed to suit right-hand movements into deceleration lanes in the central reserve of dual carriageway roads.

5.202 to 5.210 not allocated.

left turn arrows should be combined in the nearside lane. Similarly where there is a left filter arrow in the traffic signal installation the filter lane should always be marked by the left arrow marking alone in order to exclude non-filtering traffic.

(v) **Lane destination markings** (Fig. 5:37)

5.193 At heavily trafficked junctions worded lane destinations repeating the information shown on the advance direction signs may, with advantage, be marked on the carriageway on the approaches to junctions. Besides indicating the correct lane to take, the markings also provide drivers with a useful supplementary indication to the advance direction sign in the event of the latter being obstructed by tall vehicles. See Appendix III.

5.194 The marking should be normally located at least as far back from the junction as the longest peak hour traffic queues, but not before a previous main junction.

55

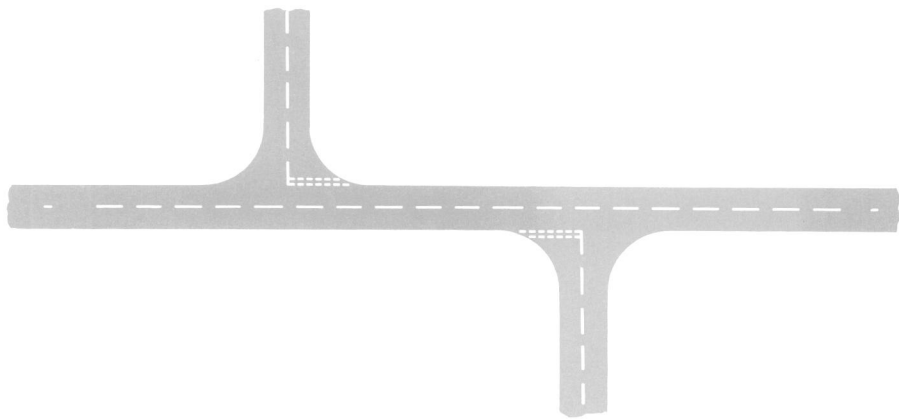

**Fig. 5:39**

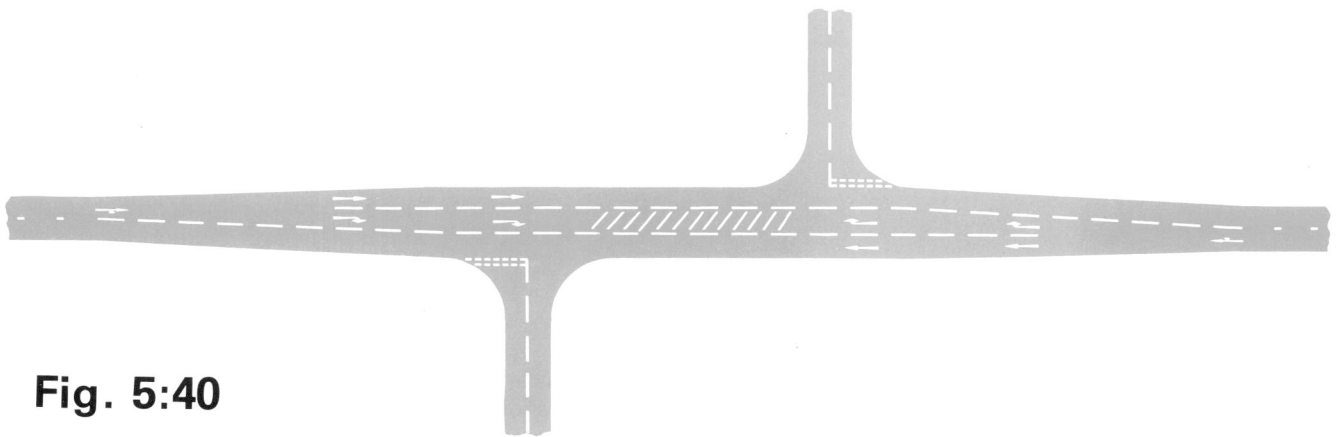

**Fig. 5:40**

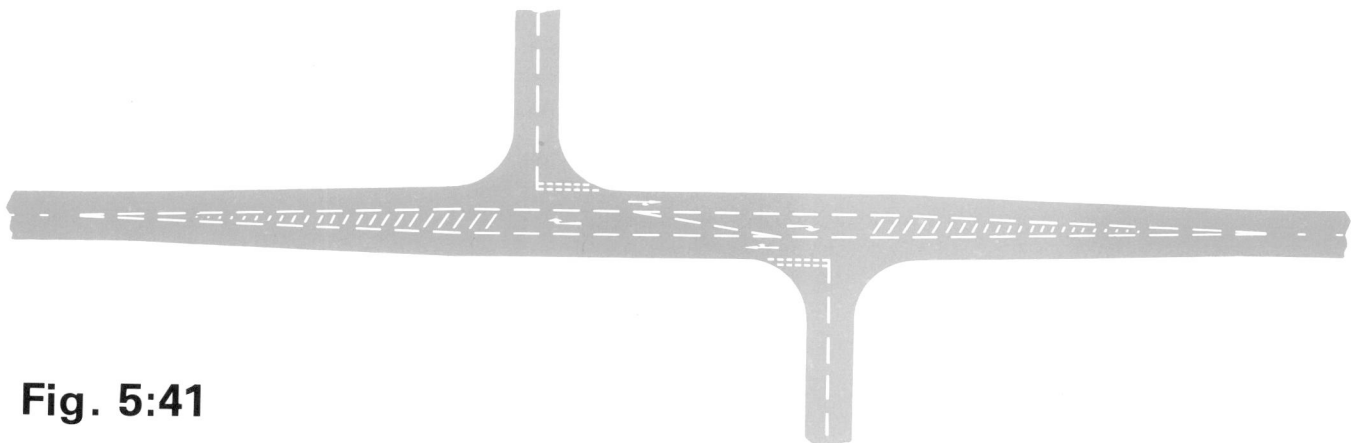

**Fig. 5:41**

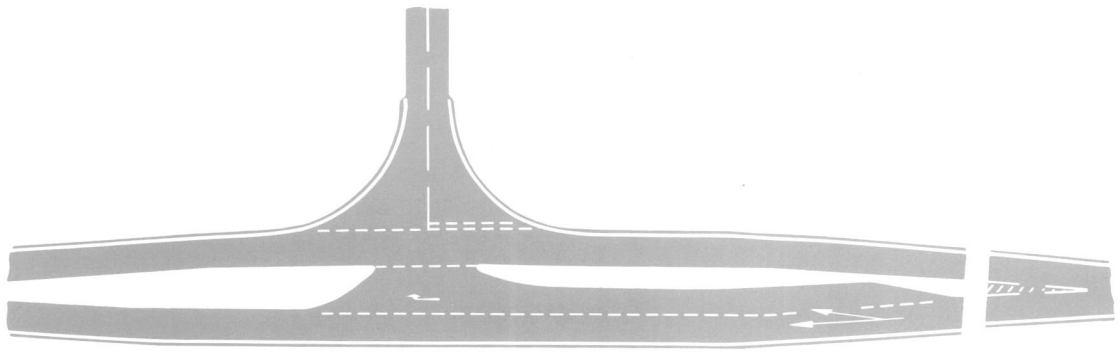

Fig. 5:42

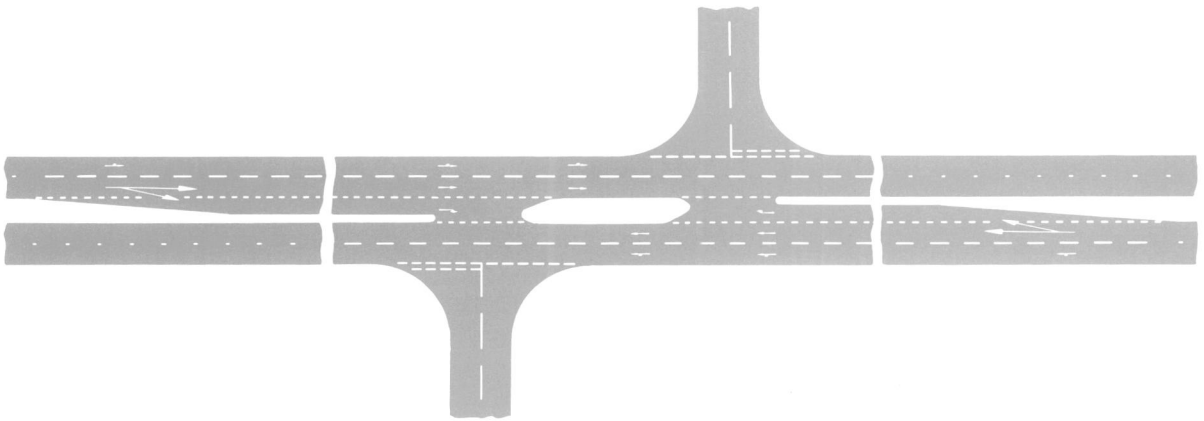

Fig. 5:43

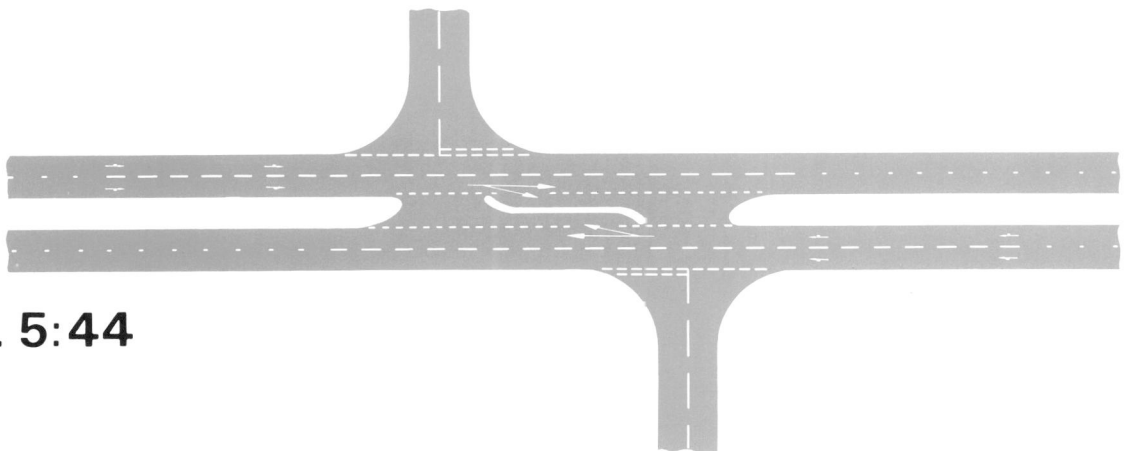

Fig. 5:44

Fig. 5:45

Fig. 5:46

Fig. 5:47

Fig. 5:48

Fig. 5:49

**Fig. 5:50**

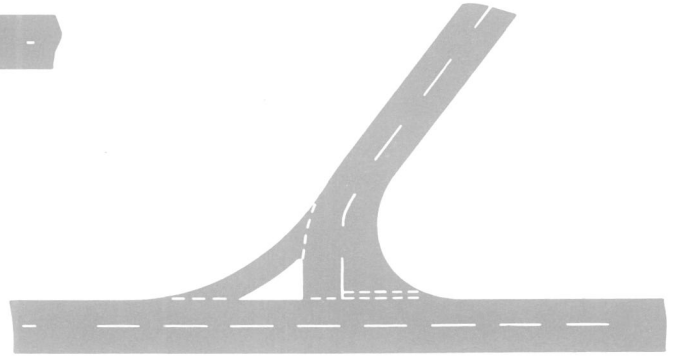

**Fig. 5:51**

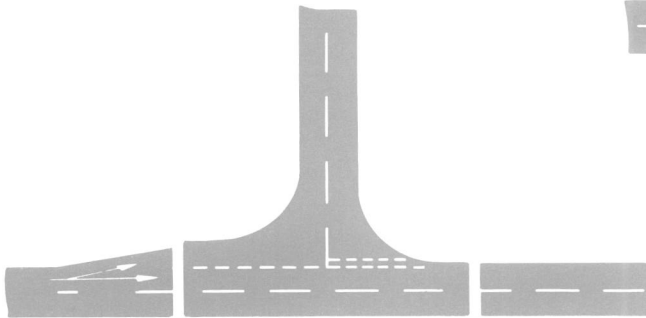

**Fig. 5:52**

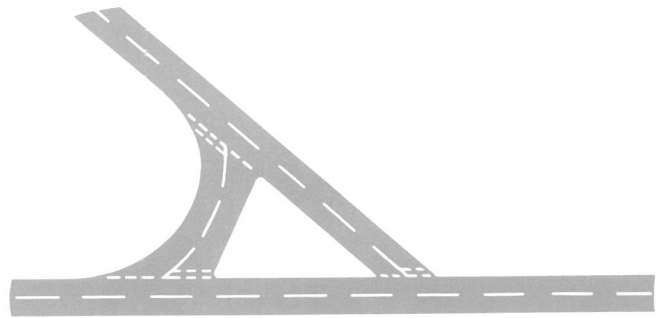

**Fig. 5:53**

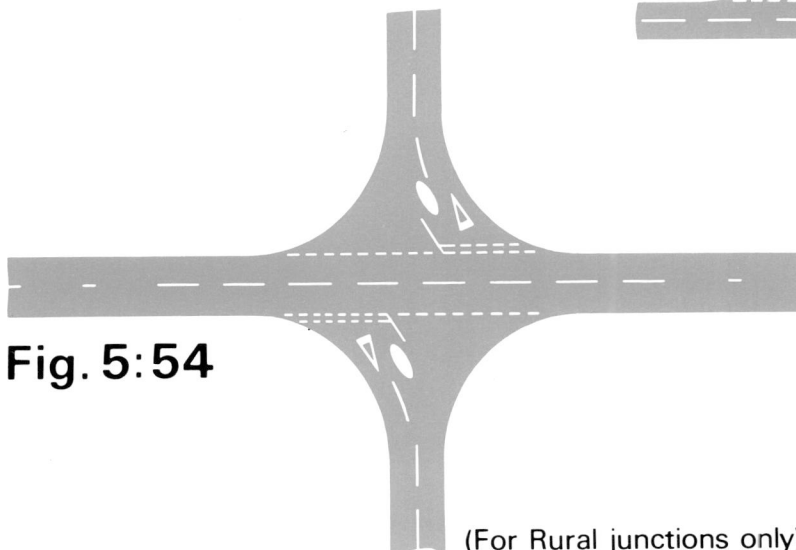

**Fig. 5:54**

(For Rural junctions only)

Figs. 5:55 and 5:56
not allocated

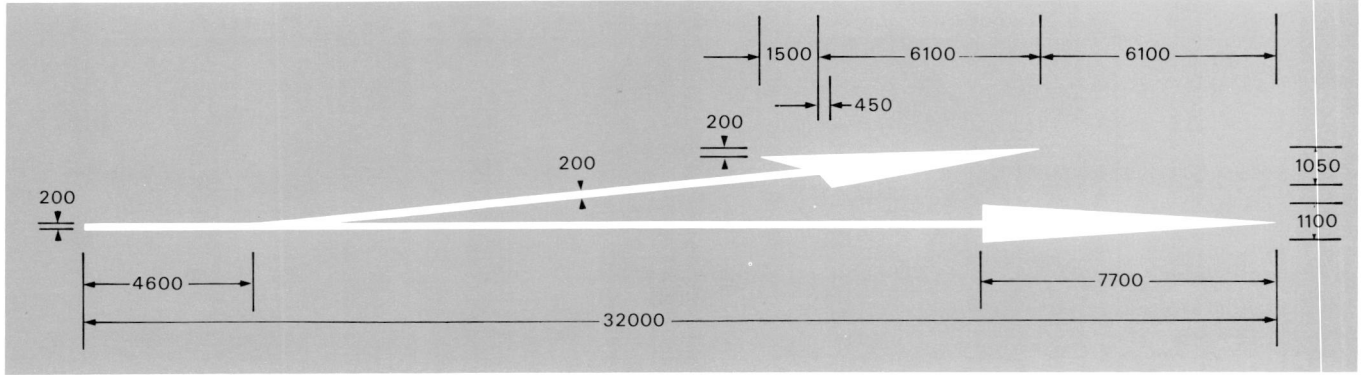

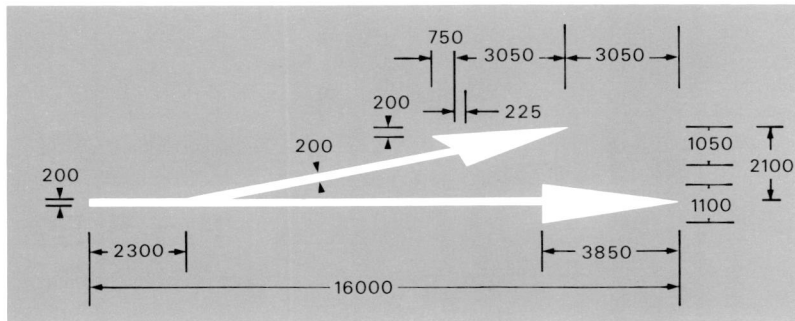

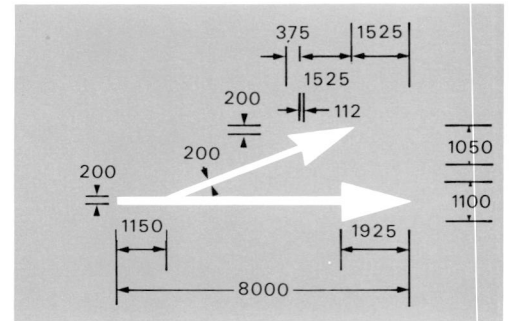

## Fig. 5:57 (Diag. 1039)
Bifurcation arrows

## Fig. 5:58 (Diag. 1038)
Traffic lane markings

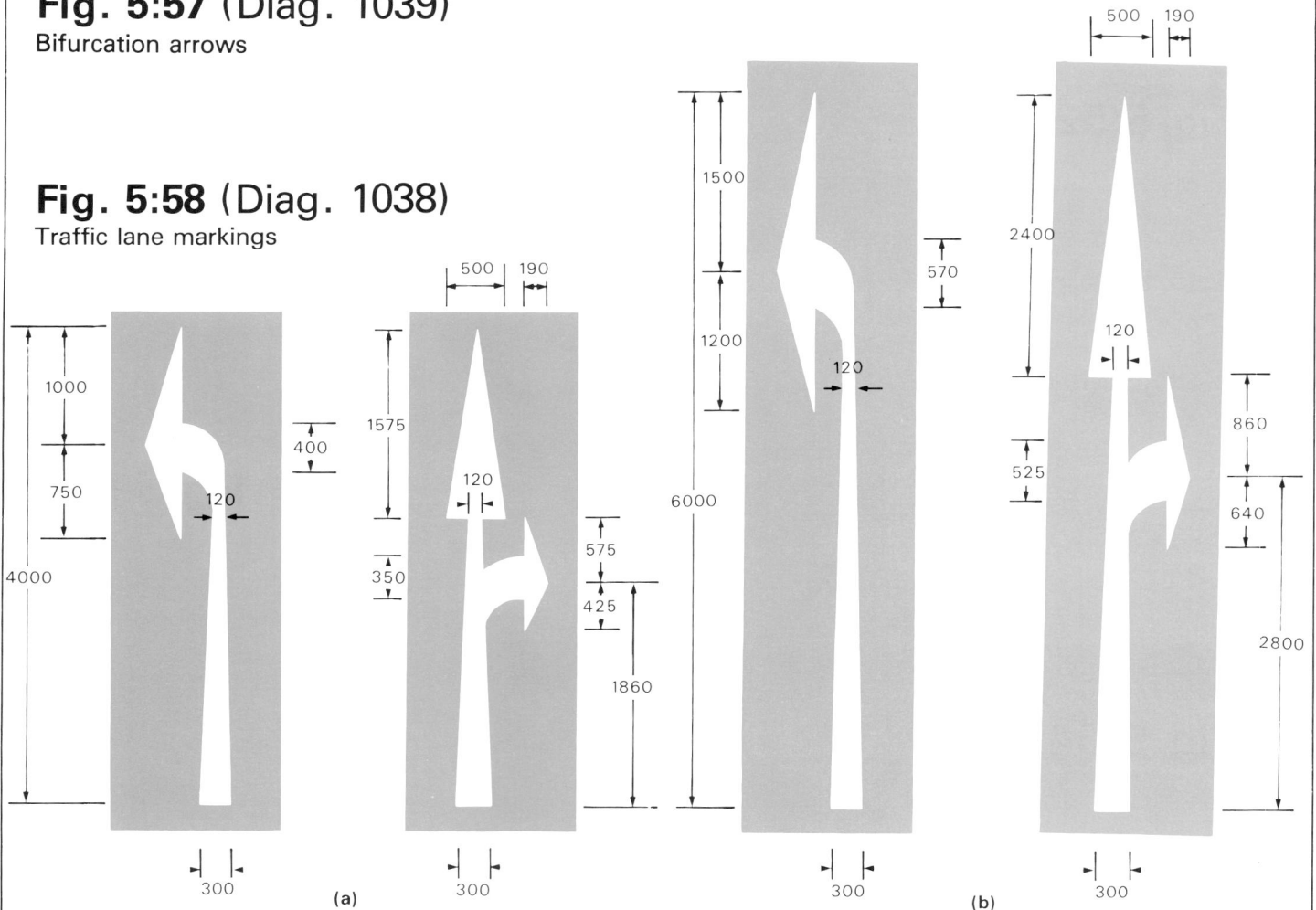

# 14. Pedestrian Crossings and Zig-Zag Markings

5.211 The carriageway markings for Zebra and Pelican crossings are dealt with in this Section.

**ZEBRA CROSSINGS** Fig. 5:59 The markings referred to are prescribed in The 'Zebra' Pedestrian Crossing Regulations 1971. SI 1971 No 1524.

5.212 The markings used to indicate a Zebra pedestrian crossing are as follows:—
(i) Road studs.
(ii) Alternate black and white stripes.
(iii) GIVE WAY lines.
(iv) Zig-zag lines including terminal lines.

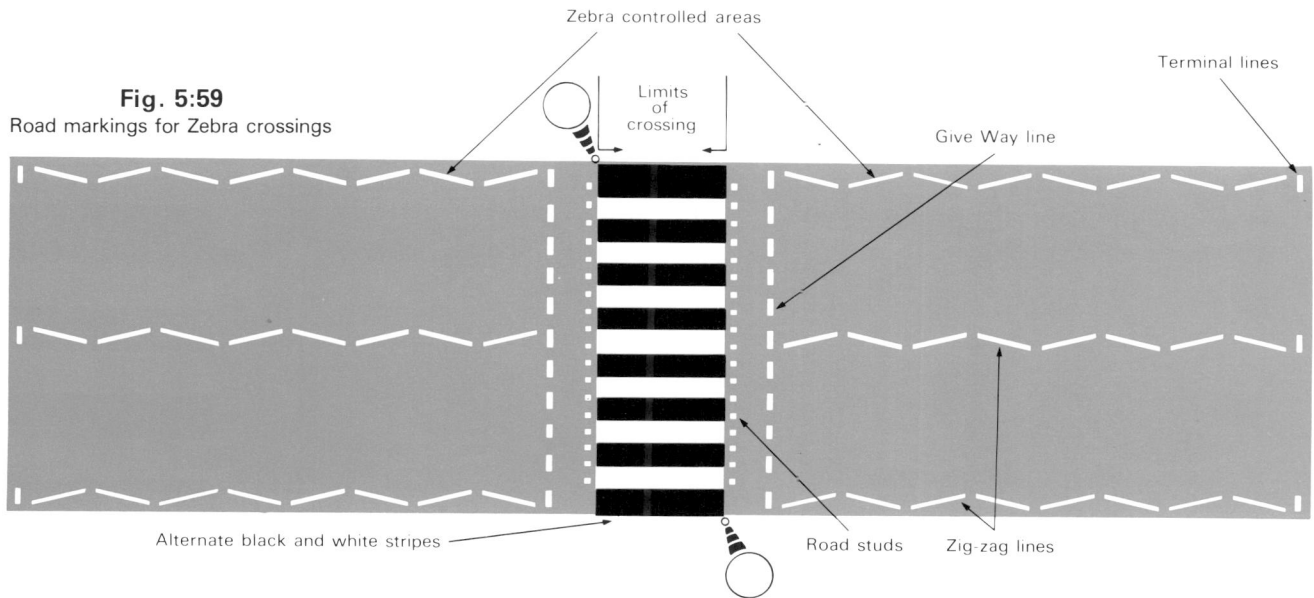

**Fig. 5:59**
Road markings for Zebra crossings

(i) **Road Studs**

5.213 Road studs indicate the limits of the pedestrian crossing. They shall be arranged in two lines across the carriageway at a minimum distance of 2.4m apart. The width of the crossing is determined by the number of pedestrians and 0.5m should be added to the minimum width for each 125 pedestrians per hour above 600, averaged over the four peak hours up to a statutory maximum width of 10.1m. However, special authorisation from the Secretary of State is necessary where a crossing over 5m wide is required.

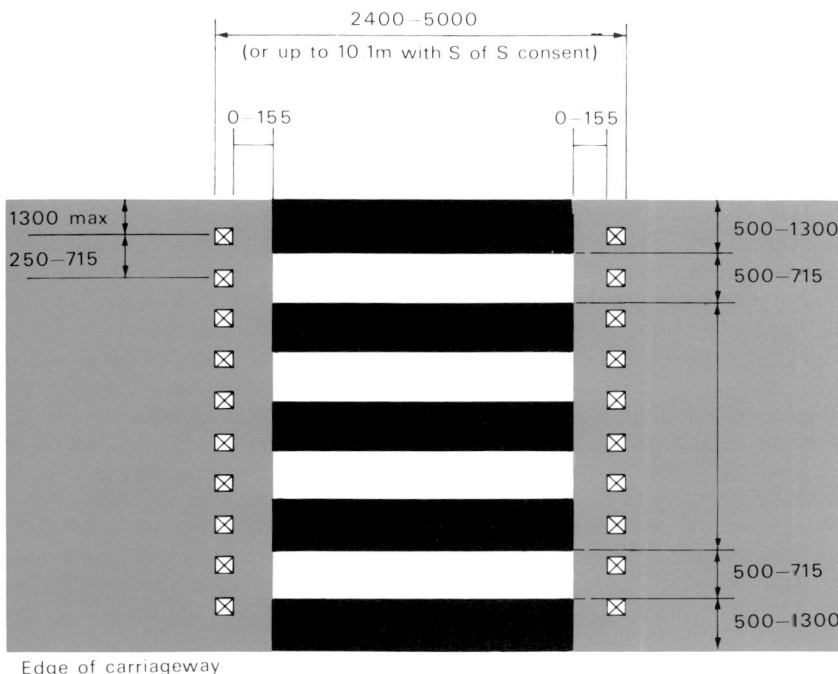

5.214 The road studs shall be non-reflective and may be white, silver or light grey in colour and may be square or circular in shape. The sides of the square or the diameter of the circular studs shall be not less than 95mm nor more than 110mm. The studs shall not project above the carriageway more than 16mm at their highest point nor more than 7mm at their edges. Other dimensions are shown in Fig. 5:60.

(ii) **Stripes**

5.215 The stripes shall be laid in an alternate black and white pattern across the full width of the carriageway and positioned centrally between the two rows of road studs.

**Fig. 5:60**
Layout of Road Studs and Stripes

5.216 The stripe immediately adjacent to the kerb on both sides of the road shall be black and shall not be less than 500mm wide nor more than 1300mm wide.

5.217 The intermediate black and white stripes shall be not less than 500mm wide nor more than 715mm wide and shall normally be of equal width.
Materials used to denote the striped pattern are normally either (a) super-imposed thermo plastic, or (b) pre-fabricated plastic tiles which are attached to the carriageway surface by means of an adhesive.
Whatever material is used care must be taken to ensure that the skidding resistance of the striped area does not fall below a value of 45.

5.218 In the case of thermo plastic material the skidding resistance may be improved by adding calcined bauxite to the aggregate content of the material.

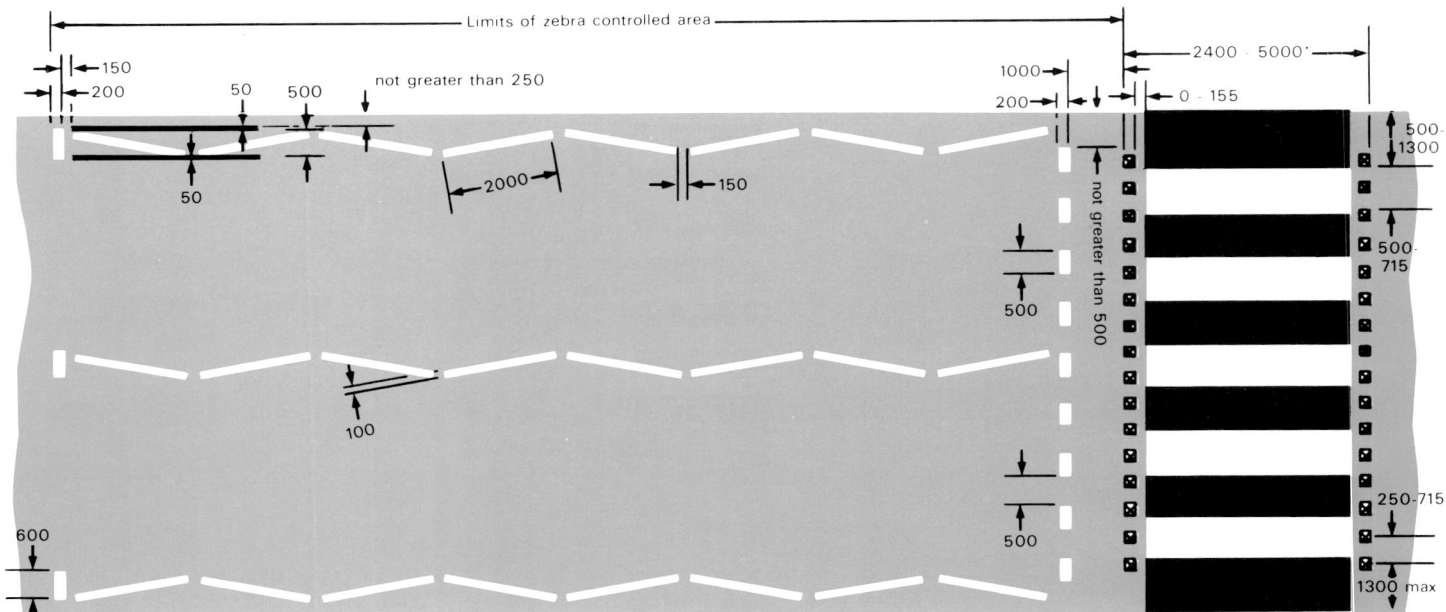

**Fig. 5:61**
Layout of Give-Way and Zig-Zag Lines

'see paragraph 5 213

### (iii) **Give Way lines**
5.219 The GIVE WAY line consists of a single broken line comprising 500mm marks and 500mm gaps. The marks are 200mm wide.

5.220 The GIVE WAY line is normally sited 1m from and parallel to the line of road studs used to indicate the limits of the crossing and shall extend across the carriageway as indicated in Fig. 5:61.

5.221 In special cases, where the angle of the crossing in relation to the edge of the carriageway makes it impracticable for the GIVE WAY line and the line of the road studs to be parallel, then the angle and the distance between them may be varied.

### (iv) **Zig-Zag and Terminal Lines**
5.222 On carriageways of less than 6m wide, two longitudinal zig-zag lines should be laid, one on each side of the carriageway with a hazard line placed down the centre in accordance with normal practice. On carriageways 6m or more in width three longitudinal zig-zag lines should be laid, one on each side of the carriageway and the third laid centrally, replacing the hazard line. However, on particularly wide roads with no central reservation it may be advisable to lay more than three longitudinal zig-zag lines to make the Zebra controlled areas more conspicuous to drivers.

5.223 The length of the 'standard' controlled area (ie the GIVE WAY line plus 8 × 2m zig-zag marks plus the terminal line) laid to the measurements specified is 18.606m. Where a longer approach warning is required, eg due to poor visibility or speed of traffic, the number of marks may be increased to 18. The aim should be to lay at least the standard pattern on both sides of the crossing but because of site difficulties this will not always be possible. In these conditions the Regulations permit a variation in the length of the zig-zag marks of between 1m (minimum) and 2m (maximum) and a reduction in the number of marks to a minimum of 2.

5.224 Zig-Zag marks shorter than 2m may only be used to indicate a controlled area of less than 8 marks. Even then the aim should always be to provide marks as near as possible to the maximum 2m length. This can be done by reducing the number of marks in the zig-zag line related to the overall approach length available on site, as shown in the following Table: —

| OVERALL CONTROLLED AREA LENGTH AVAILABLE FOR MARKINGS | RECOMMENDED NUMBER OF EQUAL LENGTH ZIG-ZAG MARKS |
|---|---|
| METRES | NUMBER |
| 3.750 – 5.500 | 2 |
| 5.500 – 7.500 | 3 |
| 7.500 – 10.000 | 4 |
| 10.000 – 12.000 | 5 |
| 12.000 – 14.000 | 6 |
| 14.000 – 16.500 | 7 |
| 16.500 – 18.606 | 8 |

NOTE:

(i) The controlled area lengths given in Column 1 of the Table include the GIVE WAY line, terminal line zig-zag marks and all intermediate gaps.

(ii) Zig-zag pattern markings can only be laid if the minimum controlled area length of 3.750m is available. (But see para 5 228).

(iii) The distances in Column 1 from which the number of marks are calculated are not critical and the lower number of marks should be used where overlaps occur (eg for a controlled area length of 14m, 6 zig-zag marks should be used).

5.225 Setting out the GIVE WAY and terminal lines is straightforward but the zig-zag marks have to be angled between two guide lines 500mm apart. In 'standard' and all longer

patterns the unit length of each zig-zag mark should be 2m and they may be set out by using a fixed dimension stencil angled between the guide lines.

5.226 In controlled areas of less than the standard length (ie between 3.750m and 18.606m) the number of zig-zag marks appropriate to the actual measured length should be read from the Table in para 5.224. The longitudinal limit of each mark related to the 500mm guide lines (X in the diagram) is obtained from the following formula: —

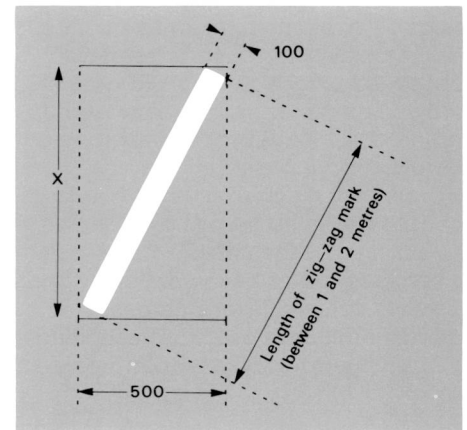

*Where L = the overall length of carriageway available as measured on site in millimetres.*

*N = The number of marks required from the table*

*Then: —*

$$X = \frac{L - 1400 - 150(N + 1)}{1000N} \text{ metres}$$

To provide marks between 1m and 2m in length the longitudinal distance 'X' should be between 0.954m and 1.982m.

5.227 The marking of a Zebra controlled area in relation to nearby junctions will first depend on whether the crossing is on the major or minor road of the junction. On a major road the controlled area may extend across the mouth of the minor road but it must never stop between the two projected kerb lines of the minor road. If the appropriate length of the standard marking (consisting of 8 × 2m marks) would produce the latter result, the zig-zags should be extended to the projection of the far kerb line of the minor road. If the crossing is on the minor road then the controlled area may never extend beyond the near kerb line of the major road.

5.228 Zebra crossings on minor roads close to junctions will tend to restrict the layout of the controlled area markings. To preserve the effectiveness of junction STOP or GIVE WAY transverse lines, the terminal line of the zig-zag markings should not normally be less than 1m from the nearest junction STOP or GIVE WAY line. This separating distance may be reduced to a minimum of 500mm to enable the minimum pattern of markings to be laid (rather than none at all). On narrow roads where the worded STOP marking may conflict with the zig-zags it will be necessary to omit one or other of the markings depending upon the layout of the junction. The advice of the Director (Transport) should be sought in these cases.

5.229 Where a Zebra crossing is on a minor road near a junction and the distance between it and the junction GIVE WAY lines is less than 3.750m plus the 500mm minimum clearance required in para 5.228, then, zig-zag markings cannot be provided. In such cases the Regulations require the Zebra GIVE WAY line to be laid, unless site conditions make it impracticable—provided the distance separating it and the nearest junction GIVE WAY transverse line is at least 1.5m.

5.230 not allocated

5.231 Normally each zig-zag line in a pattern should contain the same number of marks. But the Regulations allow for an exception to this rule to provide maximum coverage of the controlled area where the distances on each side of the carriageway between the crossing and the junction kerb line are unequal.

5.232 At crossings not positioned at right angles to the carriageway the GIVE WAY line should where possible always be at right angles to the carriageway. This is to ensure that drivers do not violate the overtaking ban when stopping at the GIVE WAY line alongside other vehicles. However, where this is not practicable the aim should be to place the GIVE WAY line so as to produce a commonsense layout, bearing in mind that its angle in relation to the edge of the carriageway must not obviously invite drivers to disobey the overtaking ban.

5.233 On dual carriageway roads and one-way streets at least the standard pattern of markings should be laid on both sides of the crossing—as on other types of road.

5.234 Where a Zebra crossing is situated on the approach/exit to a roundabout the markings should not be extended into the circulatory area of the roundabout and should be subject to the restrictions mentioned in paras 5.228 and 5.229.

## PELICAN CROSSINGS Figs. 5:62 & 5:63

The markings referred to are prescribed in the 'Pelican' Pedestrian Crossing Regulations and General Directions 1969 SI 1969 No 888.

5.235 The Carriageway markings used to indicate the presence of a Pelican pedestrian crossing are as follows:—

(i) Road Studs
(ii) Stop Lines
(iii) Warning Lines

They are used at both uninterrupted crossings, ie where the crossing is unrestricted by either a street refuge or central reservation, and interrupted crossings, ie where the crossing is interrupted by a street refuge or central reservation, in the manner described in the following paragraphs.

### (i) Road Studs

5.236 Road studs should be provided to indicate the limits of the pedestrian crossing area. They should be arranged in two lines across the carriageway (or between the edge of the carriageway and a street refuge or central reservation) at a minimum distance of 2.4m apart. As with Zebra crossings (para 5.213) the width of the crossing depends upon the number of pedestrians. A maximum width of 5.00m is recommended, however, widths up to 10.00m are permitted having regard to the layout of the carriageway and the extent to which it is used by pedestrians.

5.237 The studs should be non-reflective and may be white, silver or light grey in colour and may be square or circular in shape. The size of the square or the diameter of the circular should be not less than 95mm nor more than 110mm.

5.238 The studs must not project above the carriageway by more than the 15mm at their highest point or 6mm at their edges.

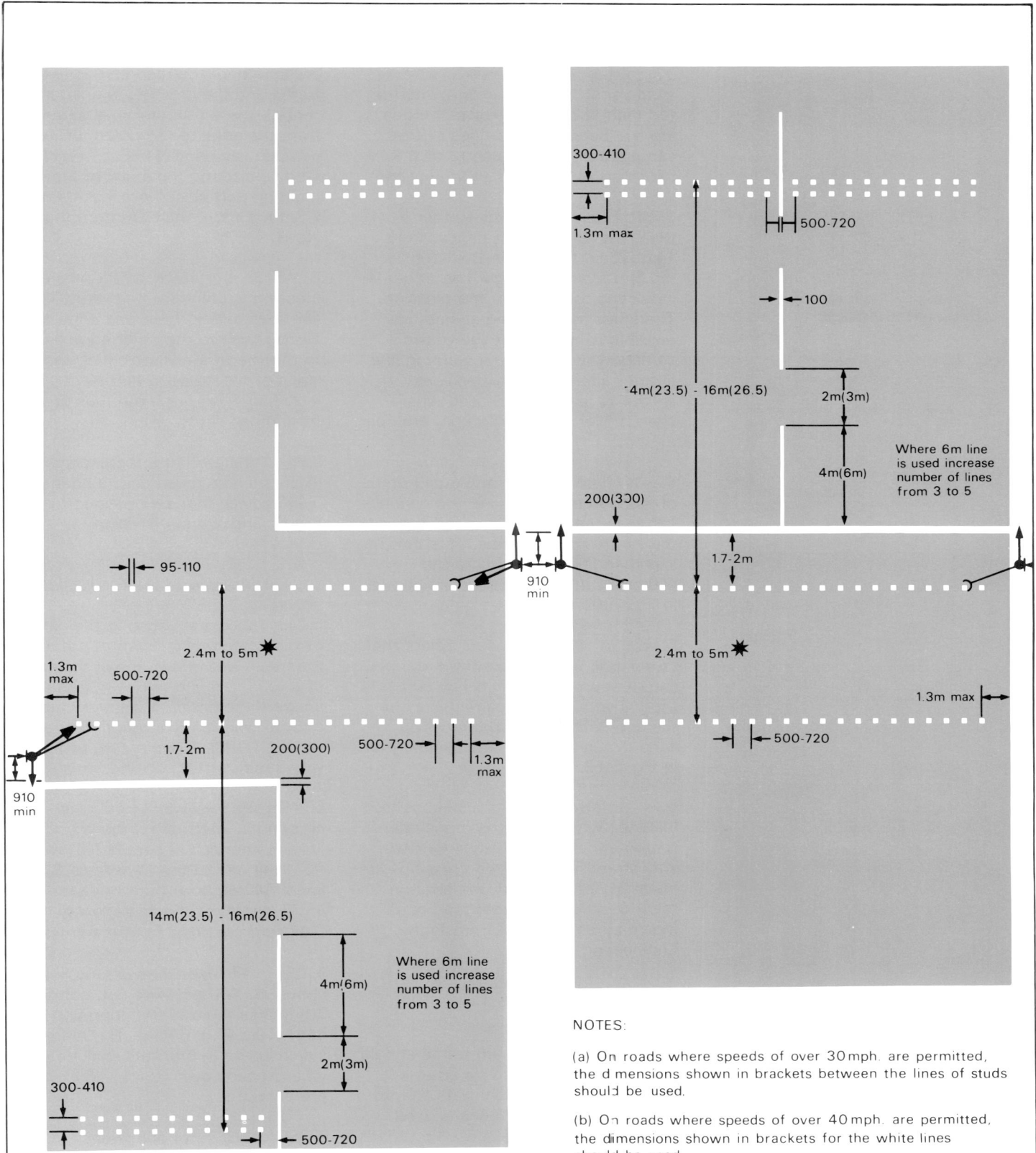

## Fig. 5:62
Typical arrangement for two-way street

NOTES:

(a) On roads where speeds of over 30 mph. are permitted, the dimensions shown in brackets between the lines of studs should be used.

(b) On roads where speeds of over 40 mph. are permitted, the dimensions shown in brackets for the white lines should be used.

✳ See paragraph 5.236

## Fig. 5:63
Typical arrangement for one-way street

5.239 Road studs shall also be provided to indicate to drivers the approach to a Pelican crossing. Where the road carries two-way traffic and the crossing is uninterrupted then two parallel rows of studs are laid between the edges of the carriageway and the centre of the carriageway as indicated in Fig. 5:62.

5.240 The row of studs further from the crossing must not be less than 14m (23.5m) nor more than 16m (26.5m) from the nearer line of studs indicating the limits of the crossing. The studs must be laid as near as possible to meet the edge of the carriageway and central warning line at right angles. The dimensions shown in brackets are used where speeds over 30 mph (50 kph) are permitted.

5.241 There must be an equal number of studs in each row and the distance between the rows (measured between the centres of the studs) must not be less than 300mm nor more than 410mm. Other dimensions are shown in Fig. 5:62.

5.242 On one-way streets where the crossing is uninterrupted, the double line of approach studs is laid across the full width of the carriageway on the approach side of the crossing in accordance with the dimensions given in Fig. 5:63.

5.243 In other circumstances, as for instance where the crossing is interrupted either on a one-way or two-way street, or staggered crossings are installed, advice about the arrangement of studs and other road markings may be obtained from Traffic Engineering Division.

(ii) **Stop Lines**

5.244 To indicate where traffic should stop when signalled to do so at a Pelican crossing a 200mm or 300mm wide transverse STOP line is used. The 300mm wide line is used on roads where speeds of over 40 mph (60 kph) are permitted.

5.245 Where the road carries two-way traffic and the crossing is uninterrupted, the STOP line shall extend from the edge to the centre of the carriageway parallel to the line of studs indicating the limits of the crossing and placed not less than 1.7m nor more than 2m from those studs.

5.246 On a one-way street where the crossing is uninterrupted, the STOP line shall extend from one edge of the carriageway to the other edge parallel to the line of studs indicating the limits of the crossing and placed not less than 1.7m nor more than 2m from those studs.

5.247 Where other arrangements exist, such as those described in para 5.243 advice may be obtained from Traffic Engineering Division.

(iii) **Warning Lines**

5.248 These are placed in the centre of the carriageway from (a) the end of the transverse STOP line in the case of a road carrying two-way traffic and where the crossing is uninterrupted, and (b) from the centre of the transverse STOP line in the case of a one-way street.

5.249 On a two-way street where the crossing is interrupted, the warning lines (as defined in para 5.250) extend from the end of the transverse STOP line at an angle so that they terminate in the centre of the carriageway at their furthest point from the crossing.

5.250 In all cases the warning lines should be 100mm wide and consist of 3(5) marks 4.0m (6.0m) long and 2(4) gaps 2.0m (3.0m) long. The dimensions shown in brackets shall be used when speeds over 40 mph (60 kph) are permitted.

5.251 to 5.253 not allocated.

# 15.   Treatment of Islands and Refuges

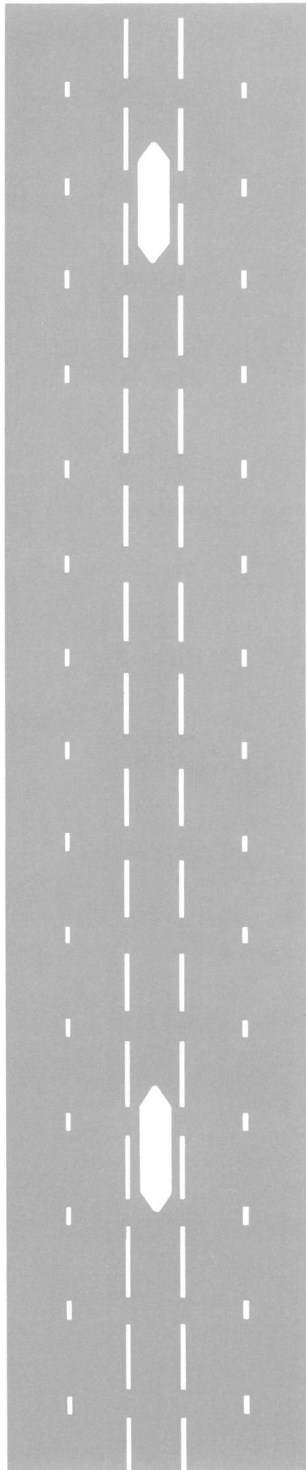

Fig. 5:64

5.254 The immediate approaches to channelising and central median islands may be marked more emphatically than described in para 5.70 by either diagonal hatched markings or by chevron markings. Both forms of marking should be bounded by warning lines to the standard pattern (6 metre module). On all-purpose roads continuous lines should NOT be used for this purpose since the markings have only warning significance and vehicles may run over them if the need arises.

5.255 Diagonal hatched markings are appropriate on the approaches to a central median island and, in certain circumstances, to an island refuge on a two-way carriageway, with the angle of the hatching arranged to deflect drivers, Fig 5:65(a) and (b).

5.256 Chevron markings are used to deflect drivers from the nose of a channelising island where a traffic stream divides. The chevrons are angled to deflect traffic in either stream, Fig 5:66(a). Similarly, chevron markings may be used to extend the nose of a channelising island where two traffic streams merge, Fig 5:66(b).

5.257 Two sets of dimensions for the thickness and spacing of both diagonal and chevron markings are prescribed. These are shown in Figs. 5:65 and 5:66.
The less emphatic dimensions are recommended for use on urban and rural single two-lane roads where 100mm wide warning lines are used, (See Table B). The more emphatic bracketed dimensions are recommended for other roads where 150mm wide warning lines are normally used.

5.258 On motorways where traffic merges or diverges at a slip road, a chevron marking of a different pattern is used, Fig. 5:67. The marking is bounded by a continuous 200mm wide line to indicate to motorists that they should not enter the area except in an emergency.

5.259 On lengths of four-lane single carriageways where a chain of pedestrian refuge islands has been provided, two parallel warning lines to the standard pattern (6m module) may be provided along each side of the refuge islands to help guide motorists using the right-hand lane away from the centre of the carriageway and thus preventing cutting-in movements on the approaches to each refuge island, Fig. 5:64. In some instances where cutting-in accidents continue to occur, diagonal hatched markings may be used to give additional emphasis to the central area but this more expensive measure should be reserved for exceptional cases.

5.260 Details of the diagonal hatched road markings, warning line and warning arrows used at the end of a length of dual carriageway road to reduce traffic to a single lane are given in Chapter 4—Fig. 4:28.

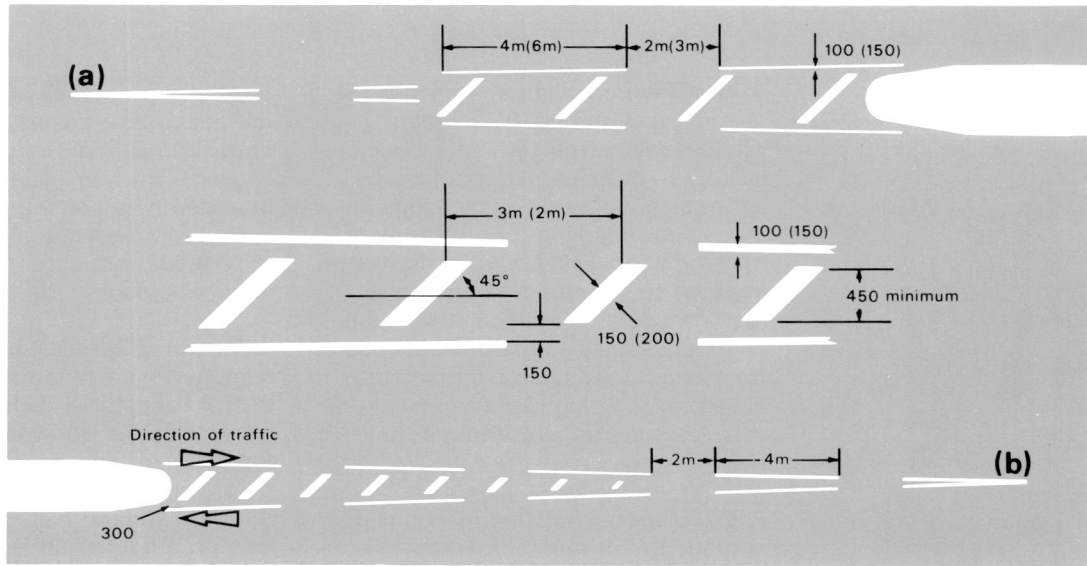

## Fig. 5:65 (Diag. 1040)
Cross hatching at approach to island

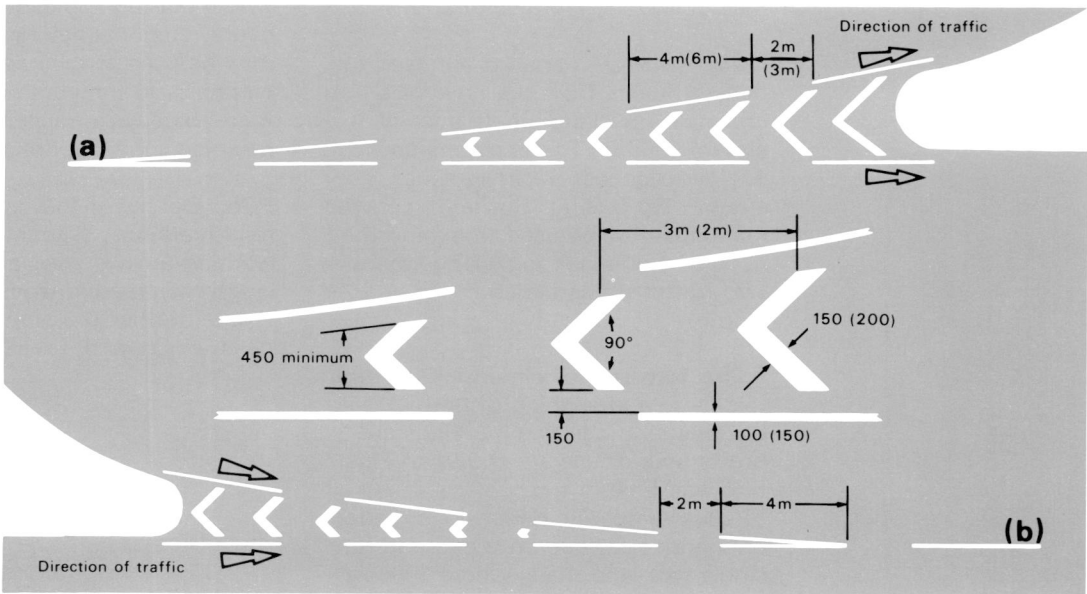

## Fig. 5:66 (Diag. 1041)
Chevron hatching at approach to island (a) diverging traffic (b) merging traffic

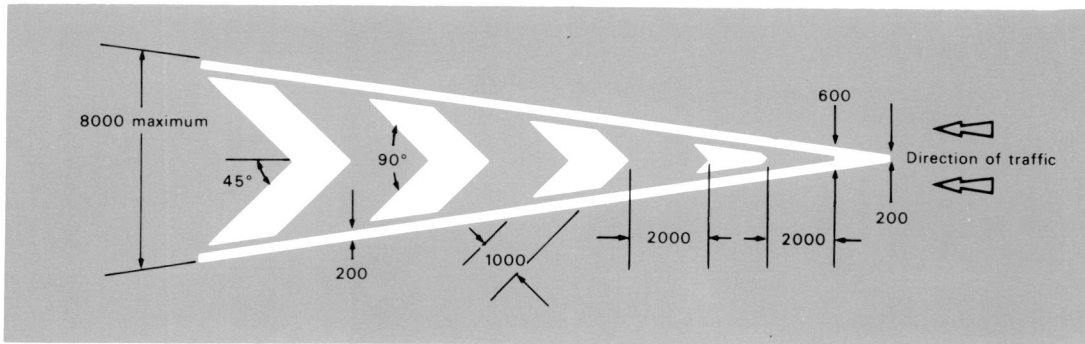

## Fig. 5:67 (Diag. 1042)

# 16. Materials

5.261 Markings are commonly laid in the following materials:

### (i) Paint

5.262 Paint is best used in situations and on roads where the markings are not subjected to heavy traffic wear. It is particularly suitable for edge-lining, for yellow waiting restriction lines and for parking bays in controlled parking schemes where the lines will not interfere with surface water drainage and will not present a danger to two-wheeled vehicles. It is also a suitable material for temporary markings.

5.263 The ease and safety in handling and the use of motorised equipment, combined with the materials low initial cost make paint an attractive economic proposition for those situations described above.

### (ii) Prefabricated Sheet Material

5.264 Markings in this material take the form of plastic sheet attached to the carriageway surface by means of an adhesive. The markings must be patterned or embossed in order to secure satisfactory resistance to skidding.

5.265 The material has good durability, is of uniform thickness and does not spread in hot weather or under the weight of heavy traffic.

5.266 Care needs to be taken to choose the right weather conditions for laying to ensure good adhesion to the carriageway surface and to prevent scaling.

### (iii) Superimposed Thermoplastic Material Conforming to BS 3262: 1976

5.267 This material is applied hot and sets on laying. It has good durability and is appropriate for use in all but the most heavily trafficked urban areas.

### (iv) Hot Sprayed Plastic

5.268 This material is sprayed on to the carriageway surface at a high temperature. It can be applied quickly and sets soon after laying. It has good durability and is most suitable for use on motorways and other high standard roads where it can be laid by motorised equipment with minimum disruption to traffic.

### (v) Inset Thermoplastic Material Conforming to BS 3262: 1976

5.269 This is also a thermosetting material. It is more finely graded than the superimposed type and is generally used at urban sites because of its greater durability. It is however an expensive technique.

### (vi) Inset Mastic Asphalt

5.270 This material is expensive but is very durable and is suitable for use in heavily trafficked urban streets.

### (vii) Non-Reflecting Road Studs

5.271 These are widely used for marking the limits of pedestrian crossings and their approaches (circular or square studs). The studs may be made of stainless steel or various forms of plastic. If the former, they should conform to BS 873: Part 4: 1973.

### (viii) Reflecting Road Studs

5.272 All reflecting road studs must be of a type approved by the Department of Transport. Reference should be made to the appropriate Director (Transport) to ascertain which particular manufacturers' products have been approved.

5.273 The dimensions of the studs must be such that, when applied to the road surface, they do not project above the maxima given in the next Section.

5.274 The studs may be reflectorised by either reflex lenses, or corner cube reflectors.

5.275 The commonly used reflex lens type (catseye) consist of a rubber insert carrying two reflex lenses let into a cast steel base. Passage of the wheel of a vehicle over the stud depresses the rubber insert which is designed to wipe the surface of the lenses by a 'squeegee' action.

5.276 Other types of solid (non-depressible) reflecting studs use reflex lenses or corner cube reflectors. The studs are fabricated in plastic material and are wedge shaped. They are fixed to the road surface by means of a suitable adhesive.

5.277 The reflectors may be uni-directional or bi-directional, and the lenses may be white, red, amber or green depending upon their position on the carriageway.

5.278 and 5.279 not allocated.

# 17.  Application of Markings

5.280 Carriageway markings may be laid either by hand or by machine. The choice will depend on such factors as the type of material, the pattern of the marking and the uniformity of its repetition, and on the amount to be laid. In busy urban areas consideration has to be given to clearing the street of parked vehicles; the only alternative may be to operate at night, or at weekends.

5.281 It is essential that all types of carriageway markings should be skid-resistant in wet conditions. Adequate skid resistance is particularly important where the camber or crossfall is steep and at junctions where turning traffic includes an appreciable number of two-wheeled vehicles. Metal plates should not be used in any circumstances because of their tendency to cause skidding.

5.282 As it is not possible to lay carriageway markings to precise dimensions and in order to allow for the markings "spreading" in service, certain tolerances in the prescribed dimensions are permitted by the Regulations.

5.283 These are:

| Specified Dimension | Permitted Tolerance Dimension |
| --- | --- |
| (a) 3m or over | Plus or minus 15% |
| (b) 300mm or over, but under 3m | Plus or minus 20% |
| (c) Under 300mm | Plus 30% or minus 20% |

5.284 The above tolerances do not apply on those road markings listed below where maximum or minimum dimensions are specified in the Regulations.
Mini roundabouts
Double White Lines
School Keep Clear
Hatched markings
Yellow box markings
Pedestrian crossings.

5.285 In the case of angled hatching the Regulations permit a variation of + or − 5° in the prescribed 45° angle. The 45° angle should be measured from the approximate centre line of the carriageway.

5.286 The method of setting out worded markings is described in Appendix III.

5.287 The following maximum projections above the level of the adjacent carriageway surface are prescribed for carriageway markings:

| Line Markings | 6mm | | |
| --- | --- | --- | --- |
| *Road Studs | Non depressible | Centre of stud 18mm | Edge of stud 6mm |
| Road Studs | Incorporating reflectors (depressible type) | Centre of stud 25mm | Edge of stud 6mm |
| Mini-Roundabouts | Central Island | Centre of Island 125mm | Edge of Island 6mm |

*The dimensions shown do not apply to studs associated with Pelican or Zebra Crossings which are dealt with in Section 14.

5.288 It is particularly important that these projections should not be exceeded because of the danger to traffic, especially to two-wheeled vehicles, and to pedestrians. Where markings are relaid over existing markings after surface dressing of the carriageway, care should be taken to ensure the overall projection of the markings does not exceed the prescribed limits. The 25mm dimension for road studs incorporating reflectors is intended to relate only to depressible types with a projection of 18mm when depressed.

5.289 Bi-directional studs are appropriate in the majority of situations including double lines, central warning lines and in lane lines on single carriageway roads. They are not appropriate for marking solid lines bounding hatched markings on sharp bends and humps; these should have the uni-directional type.

5.290 On bends, particularly where double white lines are provided, the studs should be angled so that the reflective face of each stud is presented approximately at right angles to the tangent of the curve of the road at the point where it is laid.

5.291 Although uni-directional studs are appropriate for use in centre and lane lines of dual carriageway roads, from the economic aspect, with some makes of stud, it is preferable to use the bi-directional type so that the pads can be reversed when they become worn on the side facing the traffic. Care should, however, be taken not to use bi-directional studs on dual carriageway roads at sites where they might give a misleading indication to drivers on the other carriageway, eg on bends, on lengths subject to mist or fog, or on single carriageway approaches.

5.292 to 5.294 not allocated.

# 18. Reflectorisation of Markings and Reflecting Road Studs

5.295 Where drivers normally use headlamps much improved visibility of markings can be secured by the addition of reflecting glass beads which may either be incorporated in the mix or applied after the marking is laid.

5.296 The improved efficiency of reflectorised lines is substantially reduced when the lines are wet, although they are still at least as good as unreflectorised lines. Because of their advantage over unreflectorised lines in dry weather much more use of reflectorised lines than hitherto is justified.

## Longitudinal Lines

### (a) **Double White Lines** (Table A)

5.297 These markings must always be in reflectorised materials. Reflecting road studs must also be provided. For the standard double line bi-directional white studs should be laid between the lines but where prohibitory lines are splayed to form a central island with a hatched marking between them, the studs should be located in both of the lines and should be of the uni-directional type. The stud spacing in all cases should be at 4 metre centres.

### (b) **Warning and Lane Lines** (Tables B and C)

5.298 The standard of reflectorisation of these markings will depend on the volume of traffic using the road and whether or not it is lighted throughout the hours of darkness. The following criteria are suggested for guidance:

(i) Where there is no street lighting, or where it is to a low standard or is switched off during part of the night, both reflectorised lines and reflecting road studs would be appropriate on the most heavily trafficked roads and on roads where there is high incidence of fog or rainfall, poor alignment or dangerous conditions. On lightly trafficked roads and roads not subject to fog or heavy rainfall, the choice lies between the plain lines with reflecting studs, and reflectorised lines alone.

(ii) Where the standard of street lighting is such that drivers normally use side lamps and the lighting is in operation all night, plain lines would normally be appropriate although if there is any doubt reflectorised lines should be used. Reflecting road studs may be used additionally in areas subject to fog or heavy rainfall. Stud spacing for the various lines is given in Tables B and C.

(c) **Edge of Carriageway Markings and Edge Lining** (Table D) and Fig. 5:13

5.299 (Type A). On unlighted roads the broken line should normally be reflectorised. If not then it should be provided with reflecting road studs.

5.300 (Type B). On unlighted roads the broken line should always be reflectorised but should not be fitted with reflecting road studs.

5.301 (Type C). The continuous edge line must always be reflectorised by glass beads or should incorporate crushed calcined flint. Used in white lines calcined flint improves both reflectivity and skidding resistance. Moreover its reflective efficiency is little impaired when wet. Reflecting road studs may be provided in addition to reflectorised lines on heavily trafficked primary routes where justified by the road and traffic conditions. These might include lengths subject to fog and mist or where headlamp dazzle is severe and where water is known to collect in sufficient depth to obscure the reflecting material. When used on primary routes the studs should be positioned adjacent to the lines. On motorways, where reflecting studs are always used in conjunction with edge lines, non-depressible studs are best positioned in the hardshoulder as close as possible to the lines so that the line protects them from the effects of overrunning. Depressible studs, e.g. cats-eyes, are best positioned on the carriageway side of the edge-line where they may be cleaned by overrunning. The broken edge line must also always be reflectorised,

and reflecting road studs may be provided where the conditions described above apply.

5.302 Two systems of reflective studs are prescribed. The first uses all white studs and the second uses white studs with various other colours. NOTE: Regulation 25(3) of the TSR & GD 1981, refers to the colour of reflectors incorporated in studs. Where reference is made to the colour of studs in this Section, similarly, it is the colour of the reflector that is meant.
In normal practice the colour of the body of the stud should match the colour of the reflector it contains.

5.303 Either system can be used on both single and dual carriageway all-purpose roads in accordance with the advice given in paragraphs 5.297 to 5.301. On motorways the coloured system only is used.

5.304 The significance of the various colours is based on the following principles: —

RED—indicates a line of studs which should not be crossed. They are used mainly to denote the left-hand edge of the running carriageway and only omitted at positions where traffic is permitted to cross, ie at junctions or lay-bys. At grade separated junctions red studs may be used on both sides of the nose of the entry and exit slip roads. At lay-bys on roads where edge-lining and red reflecting studs are used, it may be advantageous to continue the edge-line and studs around the back of the lay-by. However, this should only be necessary where there is a possibility of the lay-by being mistaken for a road junction in adverse weather conditions.

AMBER—indicates a line of studs which should not be crossed. They are used to denote the edge of the central reservation on dual carriageway roads and will indicate to the driver the right-hand edge of the running carriageway.

GREEN—indicates a length along the right or left-hand edge of the carriageway which may be crossed. On the left-hand side of both single and dual carriageways they are used across the mouths of junctions and at lay-bys. They are not used however in conjunction with STOP and GIVE WAY transverse markings. (See paragraph 5.306). On dual carriageways they are used in some cases across gaps in the central reserve.

WHITE—indicates a traffic lane or centre of carriageway marking and may be crossed.

## Single Carriageways

5.305 Where reflective studs are used on single carriageway roads the systems are as follows: —

(i) White only—reflectors used with lane markings (1005), hazard markings (1004) and centre line markings (1007). Also white required with flat mini roundabouts (1003.4) and double white lines (1013.1).

or (ii) Coloured—using
*white* as in (i) above
*red* with edge lines (1011 and 1012)
*green* with edge lines (1010) and at wide mouthed junctions and lay-bys and also at bus stops in lay-bys (1025.3 and 1025.4)

## Dual Carriageways

5.306 Where reflective studs are used on dual carriageway roads the systems are as follows: —

(i) White only—reflectors used with lane markings (1005) hazard markings (1004) (including where used to bound hatched areas) edge lines (1010) at gaps in central reserves.

or (ii) Coloured—using *white* as in (i) above
*red* with edge lines (1011, 1012 and 1012.1)
*green* with edge lines (1010) at wide mouthed junctions and lay-bys and at bus stops in lay-bys (1025.3 and 1025.4)
*amber* with edge lines (1011 and 1012) adjacent to central reserves

It should be noted from the above that on both single and dual carriageways the coloured system can only be used where edge lines are provided. In all cases the recommended colours should be seen only by traffic approaching on the left-hand side of the road.

5.307 The Table shown on Page 74 details the colour and recommended spacing of reflective studs for each type of carriageway marking.

5.308 Illustrations showing the use of the different coloured studs in typical situations are depicted in Figs. 5.68, 5.69, 5.70 and 5.71.

## Transverse Lines

It is recommended that transverse STOP and GIVE WAY lines should always be laid in reflectorised material. They should not be fitted with reflecting studs.

## Other Markings

5.309 On unlighted roads the worded markings STOP and SLOW, and also the triangular markings associated with the Give Way line should be laid with reflectorised material. Deflecting arrows preceding double line sections must be laid in reflectorised material.

## Motorways

5.310 For rural motorways, the standard arrangement of carriageway markings and reflecting road studs are contained in the DTp series of drawings entitled "Highway Construction Details". These drawings specify the colours and spacing of studs in relation to the carriageway markings used on rural motorways and should always be adopted whether or not road lighting is provided.

| Diag. No | Type | Line and Gap Dimensions | Colour | Spacing |
|---|---|---|---|---|
| 1004 | Rural Hazard | 6m  3m  6m  3m  6m | White | 9m |
|  | Urban Hazard | 4m    4m 2m    2m | White | 6m |
| 1005 | Rural Lane | 2m  7m  2m  7m  2m | White | 18m |
|  | Urban Lane | 1m    5m 1m    5m | White | 12m |
| 1007 | Centre on 4-lane or 10m carr. | 3m    3m 3m    3m 3m | White | 6m |
| 1010 | Edge line at wide mouthed junctions or lay-bys | 1m 1m _ _ _ _ 1m 1m _ | Green or white | 18m maximum 2m minimum |
| 1011 | Solid Edge lines | —————————— | Red or Amber | 18m or 9m |
| 1012 | Broken Edge lines | 1m  3.5 3.5  1m | Red or Amber | 18m |
| 1012.1 | Solid edge where hard shoulder | —————————— | Red or Amber | 18m or 9m |
| 1013.1 | Double White lines | 1m 5m _ 1m 5m _ | White | 4m |
| 1025.2 1025.3 | Bus Stops in lay-bys | 1m 1m _ _ _ _ 1m 1m _ | Green | 2m minimum |
| 1003.4 | Mini-roundabouts |  | White | 6 studs per island |
| 1040 1040.1 1041 | Hatched Nosings | 4m (6m)        2m (3m) | White or Red | 6m (9m) |
| 1042 | Motorway Nosings |  | Red | 3m |

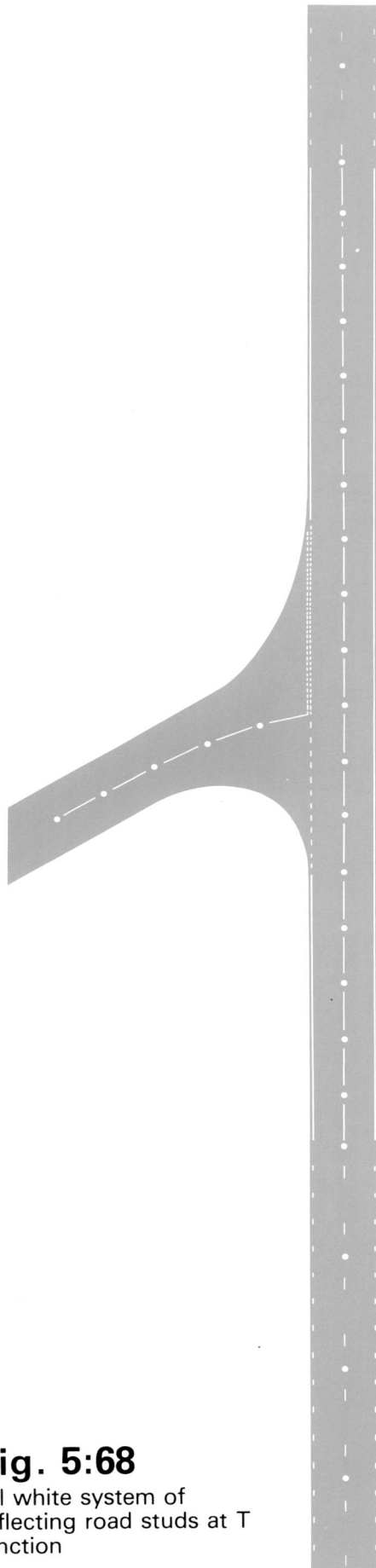

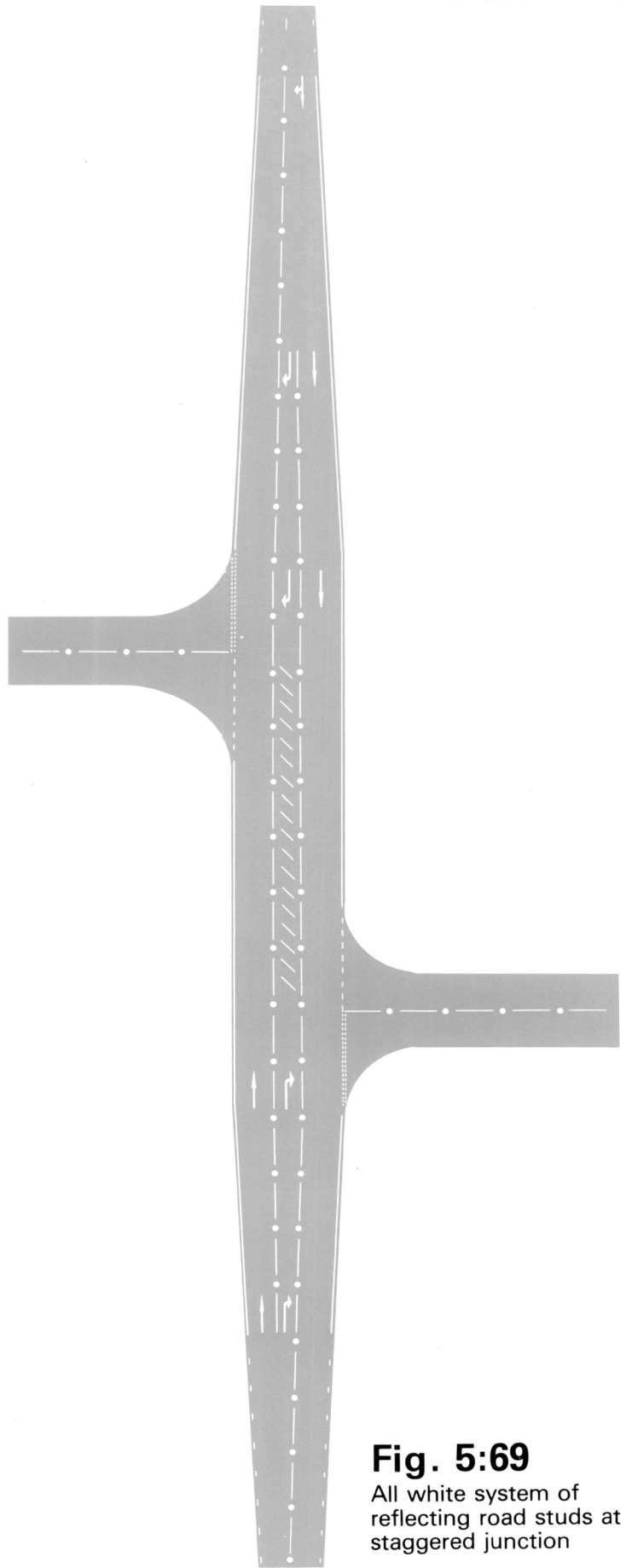

## Fig. 5:68
All white system of reflecting road studs at T junction

## Fig. 5:69
All white system of reflecting road studs at staggered junction

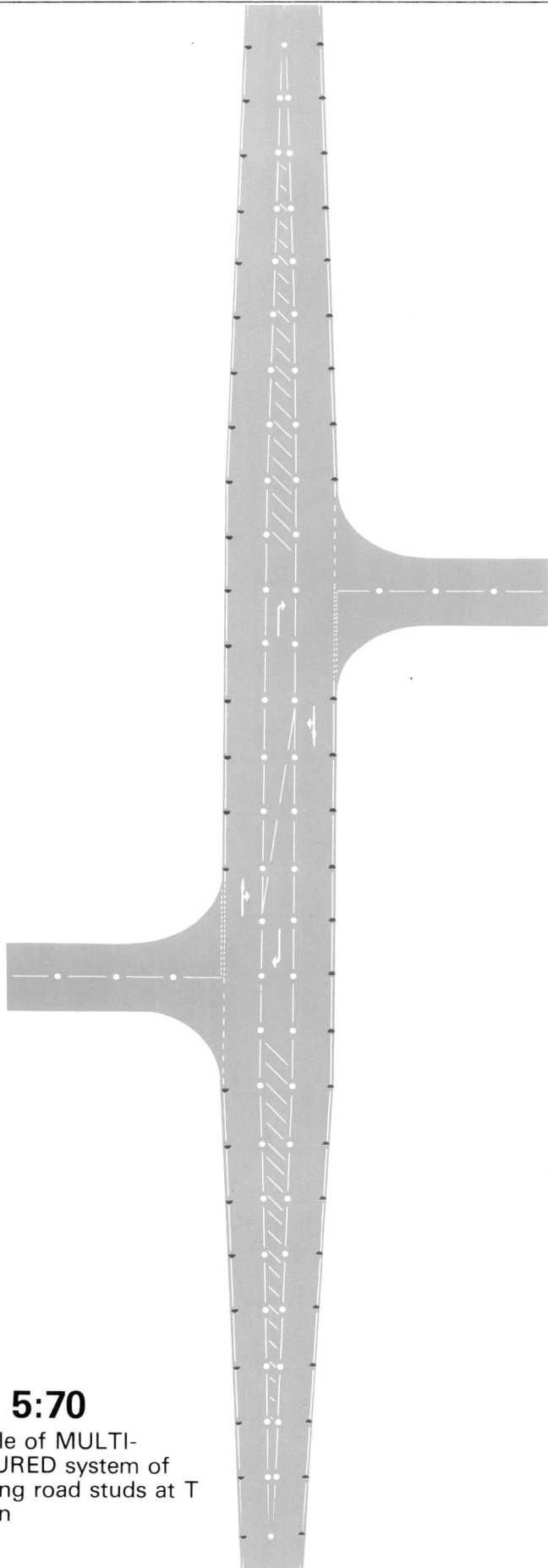

## Fig. 5:70

Example of MULTI-COLOURED system of reflecting road studs at T junction

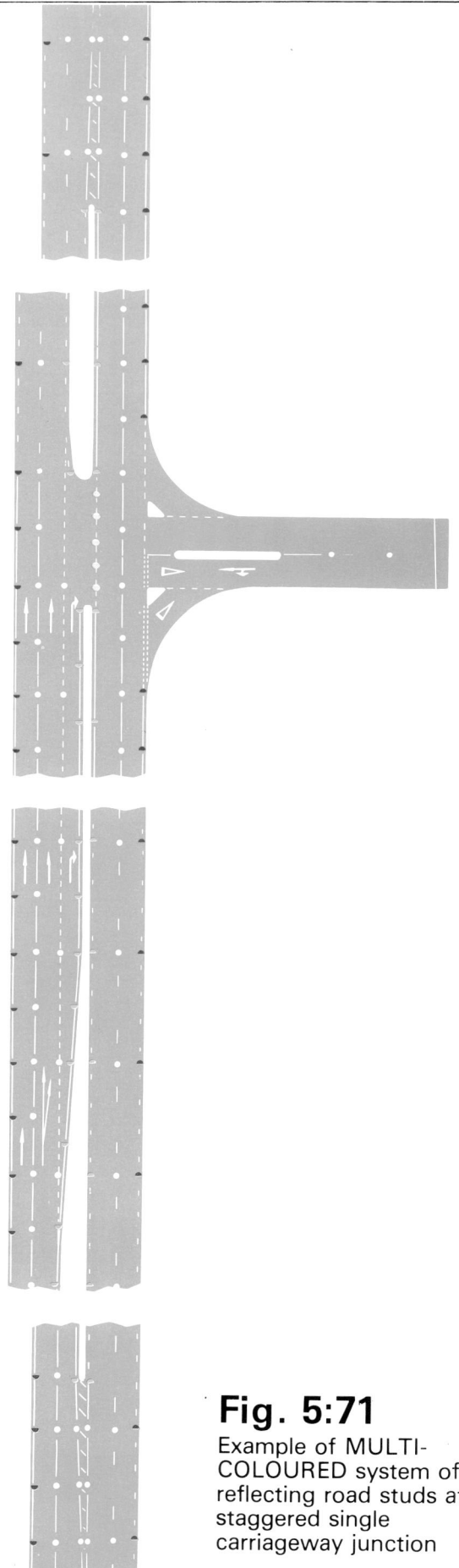

## Fig. 5:71

Example of MULTI-COLOURED system of reflecting road studs at staggered single carriageway junction

# 19. Maintenance

5.311 A high standard of maintenance of carriageway markings, including reflecting studs, is essential if they are to fulfil their purpose.

5.312 All markings including reflecting road studs, should be inspected at regular and frequent intervals both by day, and when appropriate, for reflectance at night. They should be renewed as necessary. Special checks should be made after resurfacing of the carriageway so that remedial action may be taken if required to ensure that the efficiency of the markings is not impaired.

5.313 It is not possible to recommend suitable renewal intervals for markings as these will depend very much on the type of line, the material comprising the marking and on the road traffic conditions. Highway Authorities should nevertheless keep their carriageway marking programme under constant review to ensure that the markings are maintained at a high state of efficiency at all times, particularly on heavily trafficked roads.

5.314 Markings should be renewed or relaid as soon as possible after resurfacing or on the completion of roadworks which may have interfered with them. Ideally the restoration of permanent markings should be made obligatory under the terms of the road works contract. Where it is not possible to restore them immediately in permanent materials, a temporary marking should be used, particularly at sites, such as road junctions, where the absence of the markings is likely to give rise to dangerous conditions. Arrangements should be made to protect road studs during surface dressing operations.

5.315 Where it is not possible to provide temporary road markings, drivers should be informed of their absence by means of advance warning signs. On lengths of road where lane lines or centre of carriageway lines have been removed, a sign bearing the legend 'NO ROAD MARKINGS FOR X MILES' should be used with the appropriate distance inserted. At junctions where all, or any part, of the STOP or GIVE WAY markings have been removed and temporary markings cannot be provided, a sign bearing the legend 'STOP MARKINGS ERASED' or 'GIVE WAY MARKINGS ERASED' should be placed at or near the junction preferably about 5–10m from the edge of the main road carriageway. Where road markings associated with a railway level crossing are absent then, a sign bearing the legend 'NO ROAD MARKINGS AT LEVEL CROSSING' should be used.

5.316 All obsolete markings, particularly those which may give a misleading indication, should be permanently obliterated or removed as soon as possible.

# APPENDIX I  Method of determining speed (85 Percentile Speed)

The first thing required is to ascertain the speed values at the approaches to all bends and humps where visibility might be below the warning criterion. This speed is that which is not exceeded by 85% of drivers on a dry road and under normal free flow conditions, ie when not in groups of vehicles. It is not to be assumed to be the same throughout a length of road, but is to be measured for each approach. The speed will often depend on the nature of the road preceding the immediate approach, eg the approach to the second bend of a double one will often be slower than that to the first. The speed value makes a big difference to the amount of prohibitory or warning line required, because it affects not only the lengths but also the number of places where they are required. In order to win and retain drivers respect for these lines all prohibitory and warning lines should be kept as short as possible; where there is doubt they should be left out. At the same time, for safety reasons they should not be omitted where the criteria clearly require them. Hence the speed measurements and their accuracy are very important.

Where the 85 percentile speed comes between two of the speeds quoted in paras 5.42 and 5.61 the higher figure should be adopted. For example, where the 85 percentile speed as measured is, say 40 mph (65 kph) or 41 mph (66 kph), the visibility for 43 mph (60 kph) should be used rather than that for 37 mph (70 kph).

A method by which these speeds could be measured was given in earlier editions of Chapter 5. This method gave satisfactory results but often proved difficult to apply. New and more detailed advice on speed measurement is now available and is contained in Department of Transport Advice Note TA 22/81 (Vehicle Speed Measurement on All Purpose Roads). The methods described therein and the techniques for analysing results should be used for all future double white line and warning line surveys.

# APPENDIX II   Method of determining Visibility Distances

The survey of visibility distances should be done when trees and hedges are in full foliage (or some allowance made for that). At the same time growth which obstructs visibility should be properly trimmed and lopped; this will not only make conditions better for road users, but will result in an appreciable economy in the prohibitory and warning lines, though it follows that subsequent growth must be kept well trimmed. Three methods of surveying the visibility distances which have been used successfully are described in some detail, but all of them consist of setting two observers at the required visibility distance apart and moving them forward at this set distance until a reference mark carried by the leader disappears.

When surveying visibility distances it is important that the sight lines should not be confined within the highway boundary. Such risks as tall crops for comparatively short periods should be accepted.

The common feature of all the methods is that two observers set themselves on the centre line of the road in advance of the bend or hump at the appropriate visibility distance apart and move forward, marks being made on the carriageway by the appropriate observer as a reference mark carried by the other observer disappears and re-appears.

## Method I

Two men A and B are equipped with walkie-talkie apparatus. At the approach to a right-hand bend which is likely to require prohibitory markings they get into the centre of the road and space themselves apart by the prohibitory distance appropriate to the speed of that approach, gauging this in most cases from the existing reflecting studs.

They then walk towards the bend, B leading say, A counts the studs audibly as he comes to them and B ahead adjusts his pace so that the two keep a uniform distance apart. B has a white band (tape is convenient) across his back 1.05 metres above the ground. A carries a stick of the same height. From time to time A dips and views B's band from the height of his stick. When B's band is just disappearing A calls 'halt' and A marks his position 'A1'. They then proceed at the same spacing until B's band again comes into view, when A marks his position 'A2'. Points A1 and A2 give the beginning and end of the continuous line for the direction of travel used by the team. They then reverse their functions, adjust their distance apart to the new approach speed and repeat in the opposite direction, B now trailing. He marks the position where A's white band disappears as 'B1'. Then A goes forward to adjust their spacing to the 'warning' distance which will be appropriate because they are now dealing with a left-hand exit. They proceed at the new spacing until A's white band comes into view, when B marks his position 'B2' and points B1 and B2 give the beginning and end of the continuous line for the reverse direction of travel. If the site is one which will be marked by a warning line, only the points where the visibility is first lost need to be marked. Thus, after A has marked A1, the team adjust their spacing to that appropriate for the speed in the opposite direction and when B's band comes into sight again at the new spacing B marks B1. The warning line extends between A1 and B1.

For his personal protection, each member of the Survey Team should wear a high visibility garment. A Road Works warning sign (Diagram 564) with a supplementary plate *SURVEYING* (Diagram 563) should be placed at the roadside in advance of the survey site at the siting distances recommended in Chapter 4 and this should be followed by a *ROAD NARROWS* warning sign (Diagram 517). On roads where the 85 percentile speed of private cars is over 40 mph, there should be a third sign assembly in advance of the survey site, *ROAD NARROWS* (Diagram 517) with a Single File Traffic plate (Diagram 518). The sign sizes should be as recommended in Chapter 4. At both ends of the survey site, traffic should be directed to the left by the use of two *KEEP LEFT* signs (Diagram 610) placed back to back. These signs should be accompanied by a High Intensity Flashing beacon conforming to Regulation 28. The sign sizes should be as recommended in Chapter 3. Two lines of cones or cylinders (Diagram 577 or 578) should be placed equally distant from the centre line of the carriageway throughout the length of the survey site to protect the Surveyors. Wherever possible the two lines of cones should be at least 1.5 metres apart. Traffic speed past the survey site may need to be restricted to an acceptable level. Advice about techniques for speed reduction can be obtained from the Department.

## Method II

This method is an adaptation of the previous method which materially speeds up the survey work and makes it much easier for the observers. Each of the observers A and B mentioned above is provided with walkie-talkie equipment and a small trolley which incorporates the following features:—

(a) A closed box body supported by 'C' springs on a pair of axles with pneumatic tyred wheels.

(b) A hinged lid facing the operator and consisting of a framed perspex panel, surmounts an instrument board on which are mounted at the nearside plan rollers to hold a strip map which can have the relevant information as to 85 percentile speeds of approach to each hazard and visibility distances to be used, and these rollers can be rotated by handles projecting from the body. On the offside there is a dial with a pointer moved by suitable gearing from one of the wheels for distance measurement.

(c) Two mirrors and a target are mounted on an offset bracket which is mounted on the offside of the body and fitted with a clamp. The mirrors are adjustable to enable the rear operator to sight from 1.05 metres on the periscope principle without bending and the target is also adjustable so that it can be arranged with its centre 1.05 metres above the road. It is offset, so that the target is visible to the rear operator when the forward operator is pushing his trolley. A rear view mirror to enable the operators to see what is happening behind them is provided.

**Method III**

This is simply a further development of the other two and is the fastest of the three. It uses walkie-talkie equipment and two light vans with warning signs on them. Care must be taken in the choice of the vans to ensure that the bottom of the windscreen is less than 1.05 metres above the road level, as a strip of tape is stuck on the windscreen on the passengers side so that its top edge is the required height above the road level and is used for sighting onto a target on the rear of the leading vehicle. Speedometer cables rotate a fixed number of times per mile (Km) travelled and this varies from about 800 (500) to 1,500 (930) for various types of vehicle. If, therefore, a revolution counter is attached to the speedometer cable, each number on the counter represents a distance travelled of between about 3½ft (1.075 metres) and 6½ft (1.981 metres) depending on the vehicle used. There is available on the market a splitter gearbox which, when attached near the take-off point for the speedometer drive, divides the drive into two, so that one can go to the ordinary speedometer and the other to a revolution counter mounted

near the sighting tape on the passenger's side of the van. The procedure is similar to Method I; the vans take up their positions in advance of the hazard, set themselves the required distance apart and then proceed along slowly in bottom gear with the rear observer calling with his walkie-talkie apparatus the revolution counter numbers to the leading observer so that he can adjust his speed to keep the distance separating them constant.

To avoid the trouble of turning the vans round, it is better with this method to survey a fixed length of road, say 5 miles (8 kilometres) in one direction for 'prohibitory' visibility distances and then the same in the reverse direction, and then repeat the outward run surveying for 'warning' visibility distances.

**Radio Equipment and Licensing**

Some local authorities already own suitable radio equipment, and it is likely that others will find it advantageous to do likewise. It may be practicable for authorities who do not need to do a great deal of surveying to hire equipment from manufacturers or from other authorities.

Such radio equipment must, of course, be licensed for the use which is to be made of it. The licence is not expensive but authorities should note that the GPO is unlikely to license old ex-Service portable radio equipment. Application should be made to the Radio Services Department, GPO Headquarters, London EC1.

# APPENDIX III  Worded Road Markings

1. The basic characters for worded road markings are the capitals, numerals and the apostrophe from the Transport Medium Alphabet, enlarged and in most cases elongated to two standard alphabet sizes, see Figs. 5:72 and 5:73.

**Non-Elongated Markings**

2. Some worded markings, those not aimed at moving traffic, are not elongated.

3. Examples of these are:—
School Keep Clear (Fig. 5:23)
Taxis (Fig. 5:25)
Look Left/Right (Fig. 5:28)

4. The letters for the words in these diagrams have been enlarged from the Transport Medium Alphabet to give an overall height of capital letters as indicated in the individual figures mentioned above. The length of the words are determined by butting the letter tiles together in the usual way. For ease of stencil marking or setting

| 544 | 588 | 592 | 616 | 528 | 476 | 620 | 640 | 292 | 372 |
|---|---|---|---|---|---|---|---|---|---|
| A | B | C | D | E | F | G | H | I | J |

| 552 | 428 | 736 | 672 | 624 | 520 | 632 | 564 | 548 |
|---|---|---|---|---|---|---|---|---|
| K | L | M | N | O | P | Q | R | S |

| 436 | 616 | 520 | 756 | 512 | 492 | 476 |
|---|---|---|---|---|---|---|
| T | U | V | W | X | Y | Z |

1600mm

| 316 | 480 | 508 | 528 | 488 | 504 | 416 | 520 | 512 | 532 | 156 |
|---|---|---|---|---|---|---|---|---|---|---|
| 1 | 2 | 3 | 4 | 5 | 6 | 7 | 8 | 9 | 0 | ' |

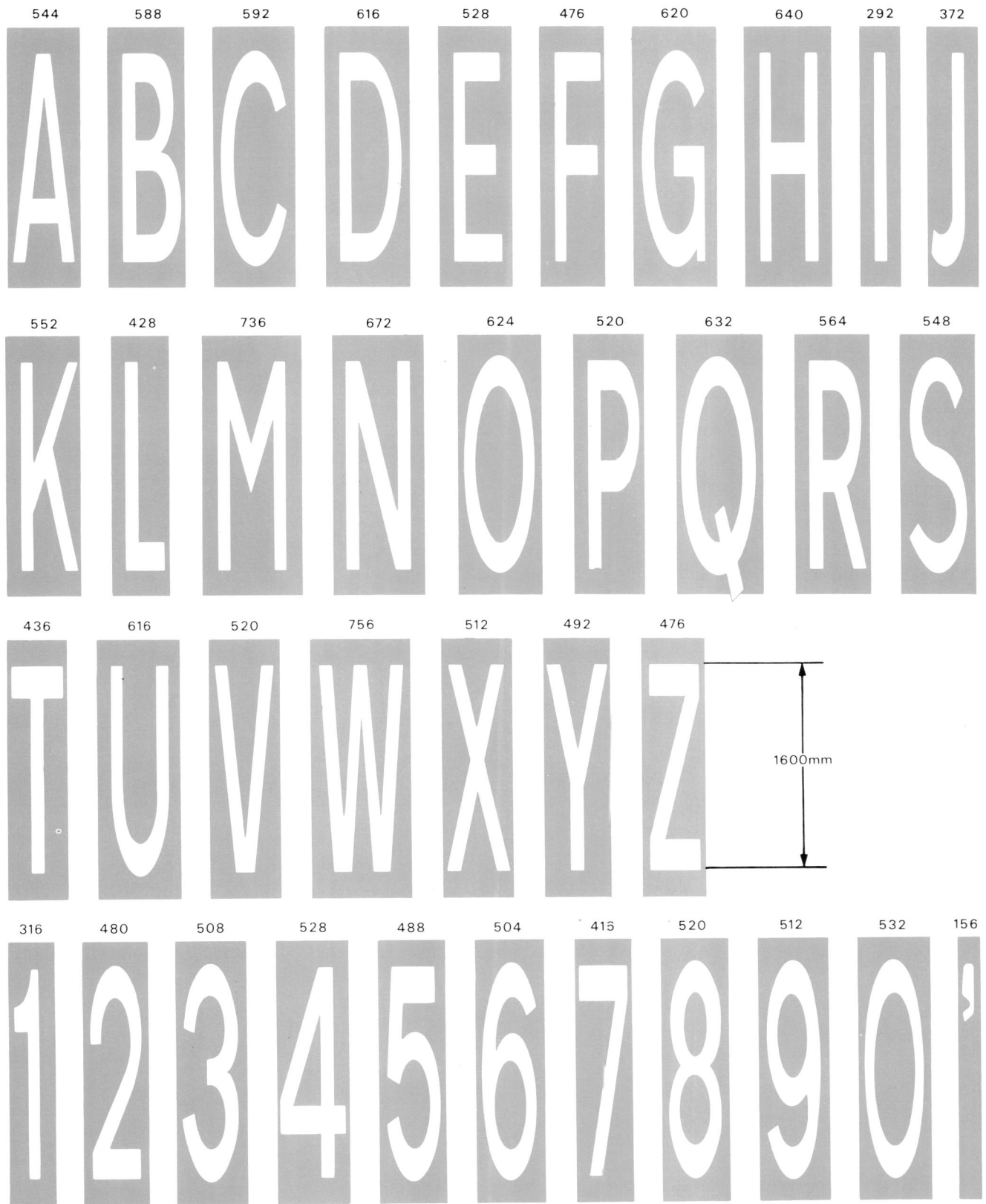

The WIDTHS of these letters and numerals are based on the Transport Medium alphabet at 400mm x-height

**Fig. 5:72**
Elongated alphabet 1,600mm

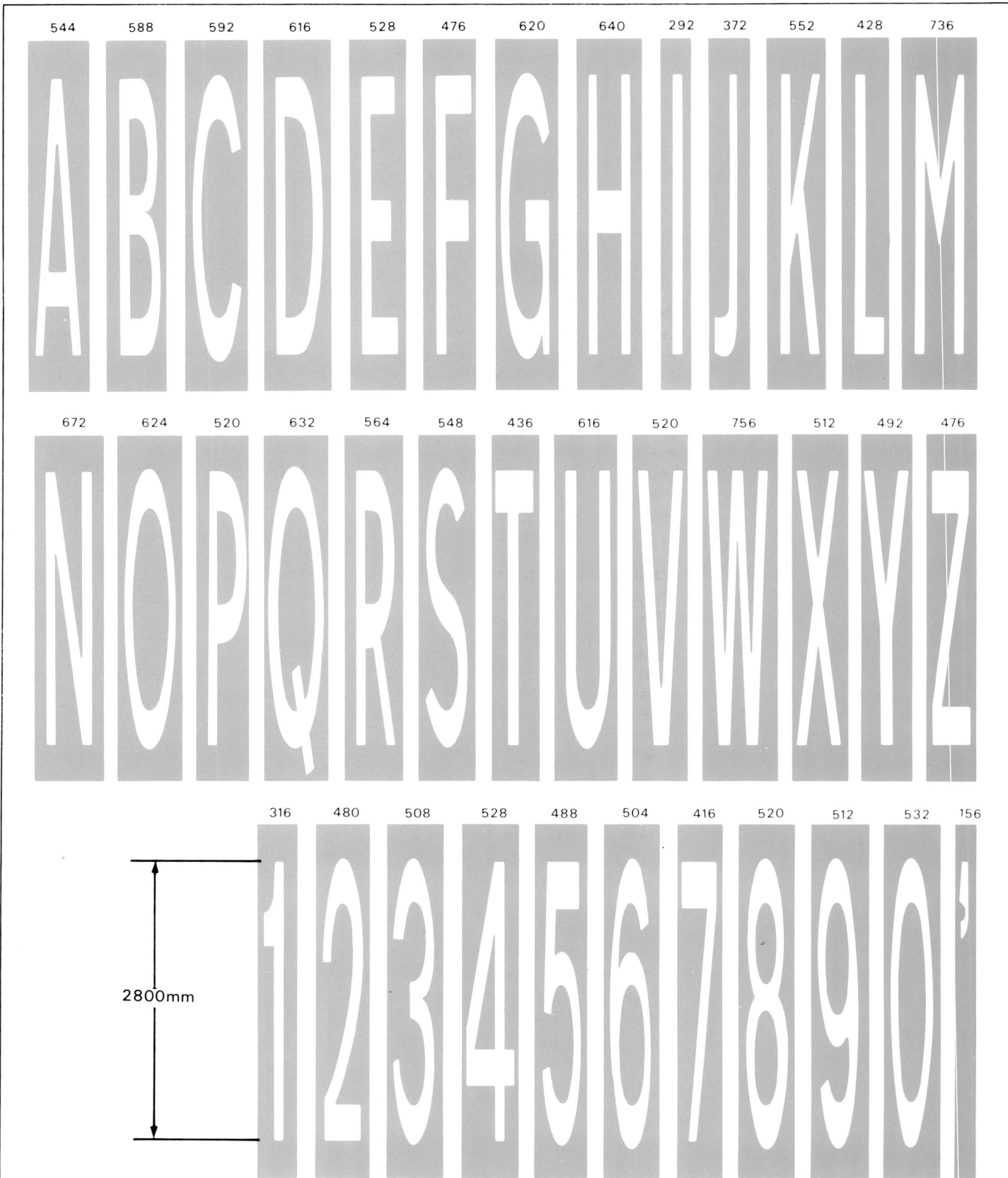

| 544 | 588 | 592 | 616 | 528 | 476 | 620 | 640 | 292 | 372 | 552 | 428 | 736 |
|---|---|---|---|---|---|---|---|---|---|---|---|---|

A B C D E F G H I J K L M

| 672 | 624 | 520 | 632 | 564 | 548 | 436 | 616 | 520 | 756 | 512 | 492 | 476 |
|---|---|---|---|---|---|---|---|---|---|---|---|---|

N O P Q R S T U V W X Y Z

| 316 | 480 | 508 | 528 | 488 | 504 | 416 | 520 | 512 | 532 | 156 |
|---|---|---|---|---|---|---|---|---|---|---|---|

1 2 3 4 5 6 7 8 9 0 '

2800mm

The WIDTHS of these letters and numerals are based on the Transport Medium alphabet at 400mm x-height

**Fig. 5:73**
Elongated alphabet 2,800mm

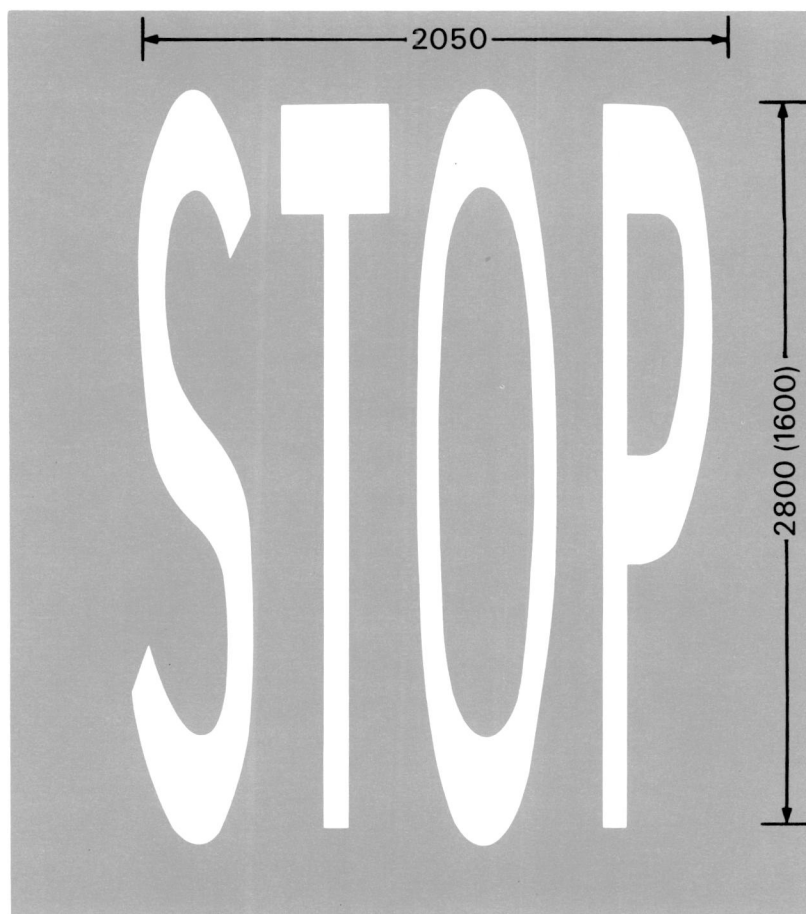

**Fig. 5:74** (Diag. 1022)
STOP marking

out the lettering may be gridded at a suitable scale. The stroke width for the letters in Fig. 5:23 is 125mm, in Fig. 5:25 is 125mm or 62mm and in Fig. 5:28 is 70mm.

**Elongated Markings**

5. An example of this is detailed in Fig. 5:74 which shows the two prescribed sizes for the STOP marking.

6. When a word is elongated it is formed in the same manner as for any worded sign in that the letter tiles are butted together. The transverse dimensions of the basic word are kept constant but the longitudinal dimensions are increased to the prescribed height; Figs. 5:72 and 5:73 show details of the two standard alphabets and numerals enlarged in this manner. The stroke width of the vertical parts of the lettering as used on the road should be 100mm.

7. To set out an elongated word marking on the carriageway the following method is suggested: —

(i) Determine how much of the carriageway width is available for the word, allowing a minimum of 300mm clear at either side.

(ii) Decide on the size of the alphabet required. This can usually be done by reference to the appropriate section of the particular marking in this chapter.

(iii) Add up the tile widths of the letters and/or numerals and determine the overall width of the marking.

(iv) If this width is less than the width calculated at (i) above then, the word may be positioned centrally within the width available.

(v) If the width is more than the width calculated at (i) above then, a suitable abbreviation will need to be considered.

**Abbreviations**

8. Should a place name have to be abbreviated then the number of letters should not exceed five. Local usage is the best guide to abbreviation, but the following are given as examples: —

| | |
|---|---|
| Bournemouth | B'MTH |
| Southampton | SO'TON |
| Plymouth | PL'MTH |
| Gloucester | GLOS'R |
| Liverpool | L'POOL |

Printed in the United Kingdom for HMSO
Dd297063  9/93  C13  G3397  10170